Devout in Doubt

PRAISE FOR *DEVOUT IN DOUBT*

In this life, pain is real and hurt hits us all. The church should be a place where hurting people can share the reality of their pain, the doubts they face, and the struggles that are real in their lives. Paul Baldwin shows how to walk through such pain and doubt with hope—and shows us the importance of being real with our doubts while on that journey.

—**Ed Stetzer,** Wheaton College

It's not often you get a front-row seat to someone who is battling a potentially life-ending disease. I felt like I was there sitting with Paul—hearing about the hopeful moments but also the very painful and doubt-filled moments. I'm not facing cancer right now, but I do face doubt. I bet you do too. Paul Baldwin has given us a gift of learning from his journey. Buy one for yourself and several copies to hand out to friends who are in the middle of tough times.

—**Tim Stevens,** executive pastor,
Willow Creek Community Church

Honest, insightful, inspiring, vulnerable, and real, *Devout in Doubt* wraps all the pastoral encouragement one needs in the everyday struggle of man living his faith. Whether you are facing cancer or a battle of any other kind, Paul Baldwin's personal journey of pain, crisis, and doubt will resonate and encourage your soul to hope in the God that loves you.

—**Kadi Cole,** leadership consultant, executive coach, and author of *Developing Female Leaders*.

All of us *go* through storms, but it's our choice to *grow* through them. As Paul's pastor, colleague, and friend, I've had a front row seat to his battle with cancer. I've watched him wrestle with God and his faith and emerge stronger than before. *Devout in Doubt* is a must-read for anyone searching for God in a difficult time.

—**Kevin Fischer,** lead pastor, Miami
Vineyard Community Church

Paul has a way of impacting someone's life when they least expect it. His walk with Jesus, compassion for others, and unwavering faith are what shine through the most. This devotional touched my heart personally because my brother is a two-time cancer survivor, and I know the struggles and pain that Paul and his family went through. Paul's words in *Devout in Doubt* are a reminder that with God, all things are possible. When I found out that every bit of profit from *Devout in Doubt* was being dedicated to the American Cancer Society, it humbled me and challenged me to do more for the world. Not only are Paul's words powerful, healing, and inspiring in this devotional, but they remind us of what is important in life.

—**Lisa Varga,** actress, producer, entrepreneur

With point-blank candor, pastor Paul Baldwin has gifted us with a deep, heartfelt devotional that deftly skips pat answers and trite responses to questions on suffering and doubt. Originally written as informal letters to friends and church members, Baldwin's spiritual and emotional journey through cancer treatment graces us with sparks of hope even in the darkest nights of pain and loneliness.

Spoiler alert: he emerges with a deeper, richer faith and understanding of the Father's goodness. Baldwin's real-life experience offers an invaluable reward for those who join him on his journey.

—**Dave Workman,** author and president of Elemental Churches Consulting Group

This is a brutal blessing of a book.

—**Abigail Baldwin,** actress and missionary

Paul has given a great and costly gift through *Devout in Doubt*: companionship in a season of suffering. Cancer is one of the great evils in this world and almost certainly every family will be impacted by it. In this devotional, Paul offers his own story—his suffering, his faith, and the goodness of Jesus in it all—to any who must walk through the valley of the shadow of cancer. If you are walking that path or have a loved one who is, I hope you take Paul up on his offer of companionship along the way. No matter what the diagnosis, you will be better for it.

—**Rob Wegner,** author of *The Starfish and The Spirit*, director of The Kansas City Underground

Paul has cared for my soul more than any other human has. If he had time to take you to coffee and listen to your story, you would sense Jesus' presence in the conversation. Because Paul knows Jesus deeply. The world is broken. We all know that. But what happens when *your* world is broken? Paul will help you recenter your life on Jesus through a simple but effective daily devotion. Allow the rhythms of these devotions to teach you how to see the Light of the World when doubt brings darkness.

—**Anthony Taylor,** pastor of Students at the Chapel

Spiritual introspection, especially during times of personal tragedy, is undoubtably a difficult task, but publishing the journey for the world to read takes real bravery. In his new book, *Devout in Doubt*, Pastor Paul Baldwin does just this as he invites his readers to journey with him spiritually and emotionally through his own cancer journal. As someone who is no stranger to heartache and has spent a good part of my career studying what the Bible has to say about suffering, I would encourage anyone to pick up a copy of *Devout in Doubt* and do the important work of taking inventory of your own heart.

—**Lucas Miles,** film producer, pastor, and author of *The Christian Left* and *Good God*

Even when pastors are confronted with a life-threatening diagnosis it provokes the questions, "Do I really believe what I have taught others to embrace? Can I really trust that God is good and cares for me? Does faith really make a difference in facing my own death?" When Pastor Paul Baldwin was diagnosed with cancer, he found catharsis in shepherding his congregation by journaling his doubts. He found inspiration from the suffering sages of the past and hope from the scriptures as he walked his congregation through his valley of the shadow of death. Paul modeled how to not only go through a life-threatening illness, but how to grow through it. He shows how to remain devout in spite of doubt.

—**Jim Tomberlin,** pastor, author, church consultant

In the corridors of history, we hear the echo of the voice of the Apostle Paul reminding us to glory in our sufferings because it produces perseverance, character, and hope. In these post-modern times, we witness perseverance, character, and hope come alive through the holy writ of *Devout in Doubt*. Pastor Paul Baldwin poignantly amplifies a voice we all need to hear when suffering unexpectedly knocks on our door—a voice that reminds us that when suffering comes . . . close at hand is the trailing beauty of the transformative grace and unsurpassable peace we all hope to find in the presence of a Holy God.

—**Charles A. Montgomery, Jr., PhD,** teaching pastor at the Vineyard Columbus and associate strategic coordinator with Vineyard USA

I am recommending Baldwin's book, *Devout in Doubt*, to anyone—Jesus follower and skeptic alike because they are very often the same person. Anyone who says they have not experienced seasons of gut-wrenching doubt is either self-deluded or just hasn't lived long enough yet. This simple book illuminates one man's real-world struggle confronting fear and doubt and breaking through to experiencing God's presence. Gaining confidence without certainty is a gift the Holy Spirit is distributing as we trust God's Word in the midst of the struggle. Who among us doesn't need daily strength for the daily dilemma of life?

—**Mike Meeks,** pastor Emeritus at Eastlake Community Church, San Diego, California

The crucibles of life reveal what lies deep within us. In reading Paul's confessions during his bout with cancer, you will discover the secret of how to be devout in the midst of your doubt. For deep within Paul lies what is most fundamental to life: community. The community of the Father, Son, and Spirit, as well as his spiritual family. When you experience love, it produces faith and hope.

—**JR Woodward,** national director of The V3 Movement, author of *Creating a Missional Culture,* and co-author of *The Church as Movement*

Devout in Doubt is a vulnerable and honest journey with God through some of the deepest valleys life can bring our way. At every step, Paul wrestles with what it means to have authentic faith in an amazing God in our world infected with profound brokenness. I was encouraged, challenged, and inspired to take up my own journey with God afresh as a result of the treasures in these pages.

—**Putty Putman,** pastor and author

DEVOUT IN DOUBT

Diving into Deeper Devotion

PAUL BALDWIN

NASHVILLE

NEW YORK • LONDON • MELBOURNE • VANCOUVER

DEVOUT IN DOUBT

Diving into Deeper Devotion

Published in New York, New York, by Morgan James Publishing. Morgan James is a trademark of Morgan James, LLC. www.MorganJamesPublishing.com

Unless otherwise noted, Scriptures are taken from the HOLY BIBLE, NEW LIVING TRANSLATION (NLT): Copyright© 1996, 2004, 2007 by Tyndale House Foundation. Used by permission of Tyndale House Publishers, Inc., Carol Stream, Illinois 60188. All rights reserved. Used by permission.

Scriptures marked "NIV" are taken from THE HOLY BIBLE, NEW INTERNATIONAL VERSION °: Copyright© 1973, 1978, 1984, 2011 by Biblica, Inc.™. Used by permission of Zondervan.

Scriptures marked "ESV" are taken from THE HOLY BIBLE, ENGLISH STANDARD VERSION (ESV): Copyright© 2001 by Crossway, a publishing ministry of Good News Publishers. Used by permission.

Scriptures marked "KJV" are taken from the KING JAMES VERSION (KJV): KING JAMES VERSION, public domain.

Scripture marked "The Message" taken from THE MESSAGE: THE BIBLE IN CONTEMPORARY ENGLISH: Copyright© 1993, 1994, 1995, 1996, 2000, 2001, 2002. Used by permission of NavPress Publishing Group.

Scriptures marked TEV are taken from the TODAY'S ENGLISH VERSION First Edition: Copyright© 1976 American Bible Society. Used by permission.

Proudly distributed by Ingram Publisher Services.

Morgan James BOGO™

A **FREE** ebook edition is available for you or a friend with the purchase of this print book.

CLEARLY SIGN YOUR NAME ABOVE

Instructions to claim your free ebook edition:
1. Visit MorganJamesBOGO.com
2. Sign your name CLEARLY in the space above
3. Complete the form and submit a photo of this entire page
4. You or your friend can download the ebook to your preferred device

ISBN 9781631957895 paperback
ISBN 9781631957901 ebook
Library of Congress Control Number: 2021947522

Cover Design by:
Megan Dillon
megan@creativeninjadesigns.com

Interior Design by:
Chris Treccani
www.3dogcreative.net

Cover Photo by:
Paul Baldwin

Morgan James is a proud partner of Habitat for Humanity Peninsula and Greater Williamsburg. Partners in building since 2006.

Get involved today! Visit MorganJamesPublishing.com/giving-back

To my wife Becky.
You are my best friend and the primary cheerleader in my life. You amaze me on so many levels! I love you.

To my children: Elizabeth, Elisha, Hannah, and Abigail.
You bring so much love, life and laughter to this world. Chase your dreams and make sure that you change the world along the way.

TABLE OF CONTENTS

FOREWORD

I have had the privilege of watching Paul Baldwin lead in ministry over the last twenty years. He is a gifted pastor, teacher, and nurturing shepherd. I, like many, was devastated when Paul shared his cancer diagnosis and the unique and demanding strategy the doctors would take to combat the disease. Paul faced a difficult challenge, and the only path forward, like is so often true in life, was to walk through.

You, like me, may never have had cancer, but we have all faced (and will face) hard moments in life, those surprising encounters where we can't find our footing . . . and the only way forward is one step at a time. The truth is that when we enter life's valleys, we often experience a refining work of God. We are stripped of all props and pretenses and laid bare for God's Holy Spirit to comfort, guide, and clothe us in new ways.

When we face difficulties, doubt is often not too far behind. We doubt ourselves, our choices, and that God really does care or even notice us. However, he does care and wants to show his extravagant love to us, an eternal love and security that transcends the sufferings and disappointments that we experience in this sin-stained world.

The recent pandemic in our world exposed our vulnerability and that we can't avoid suffering and interruptions to our own plans and desires. Jesus warned his followers (including us) about this life when he gathered his disciples together for one final time before his arrest. He said, "In this world you will have trouble."

Too often we want to ignore suffering's reality, sweep it away, or try to pass it along and make it someone else's problem. The temptation may be to do the same with a book like this. However, this devotional book is a gift to you and me, a forty-nine-day journey led by a friend who helps us to draw closer to Jesus through consistent reflection. And we need that. Whether you're going through *Devout in Doubt* on your own, in a small group, or as a congregation, you will find solid footing for the journey forward, and you will be ready for those difficult moments and the occasional doubts.

Terry Linhart, author, *The Self-Aware Leader*

PREFACE

This little devotional was birthed from my personal letters as I recorded a rather turbulent season in our lives that spanned a seven-month period between July 2020 and February 2021. On July 12, I checked myself into the Baptist Kendall Regional Medical Center in Miami, Florida. I was experiencing some abdominal pain and felt it was unusual and painful enough to warrant an ER visit. Five days later, on my forty-ninth birthday, I learned that I had non-Hodgkin's lymphoma.

Yep. Cancer. We didn't see that one coming our way. No personal history of cancer. No family history of cancer. We were completely blindsided, and our world was turned upside down within a twenty-four-hour period. Enter a flood of emotions, including fear, frustration, confusion, and doubt.

Fear. What will happen to me? Frustration. Why is this happening to me? Confusion. How did this happen to me? Doubt. Where can I find peace in what is happening to me?

Each of these emotions was certainly natural and expected. There is not a person on the planet who would not have traveled down the emotional pathway that we did. However, some might have questioned my faith if they could have replayed the doubt in my mind during this season. It's true—there was a great deal of doubt, but even so, I'm hoping you will see that while there was certainly doubt during this season, we were still devout in our faith walk, and I hope this devotional helps you live the same way during your season of suffering.

We might agree that doubt exists more on an emotional level and is really indecision between belief and disbelief. In other words, I didn't have what I needed, in my natural self, to believe that any kind of peace was coming our way to calm or appease the fear, frustration, and confusion. I needed help from something outside of myself to get that peace. Those first twenty-four hours were an emotional roller coaster, to say the least. Alone in my hospital room trying to communicate the reality of my newfound diagnosis to my wife, Becky, who was not allowed to sit with me, nor I with her, because of the worldwide COVID-19 pandemic. Emotionally, I was reaching for anything and everything that would bring some kind of sense and sensibility to this now new asinine conundrum in which we found ourselves. I knew in my heart that I needed to devote my attention to another source and supply of peace, a peace outside of the natural realm. I turned my attention and affection to a deeper and more devout faith in God.

My prayer for you during your time of suffering is that you will develop humble confidence in this reality: doubt isn't the opposite of faith; it is an element of faith. You, too, can be *devout in your doubt*. That is why I'm opening my heart to you in the next few pages. I want to lead you to that place of assurance.

My heart is for you, and I'm cheering you on!

Paul

INTRODUCTION

How to use this devotional.

A couple of simple tips to get the most out of this devotional:

The Journal Entry.

This is my story. During this season, I felt like my marching orders from God were to be completely honest and transparent about my journey. It wasn't always pretty. My writing wasn't always grammatically correct, and I certainly had no intent to write a devotional. Consequently, the narrative of these letters is quite informal. I just wrote from my current state of mind and through my own contemplations. Writing is how I process and heal in many ways.

Over the course of seven months, there are forty-nine letters that hopefully give you a picture of our story. Again, my goal is to meet you in your pain, struggle, and suffering and simply be a friend, pointing you to a more devout posture of faith in God in this season.

However, you need to know that what you hold in your hands is the product of a bit of a time-lapse over those seven months. There is so much that is not recorded, roughly another 161 days' worth, where I was either processing, experiencing too much pain, or emotionally exhausted with nothing to offer. While you'll most certainly get a sense of my reality in what is recorded, please remember that these letters were not as clean and tidy as they may come off today.

Enter the story with me and ask God to meet you there. Again, the goal is that God would use this tool to pursue you and pull you back into a deep devotion in your natural doubt.

The devotion.

There are four components to guide you following each journal entry.

1. **Quote.** I'm a sucker for a good quote. I believe God has given great men and women language to attach to our emotions and experiences. My hope is that as you read these quotes from various contributors, and from all walks of life, that your faith would be inspired, encouraged, and recharged to keep fighting the good fight of faith.

2. **Scripture reading.** I believe Scripture is the primary way God speaks to us. I've prayed over every passage selected to pass along to you. These are not my words, but God's words of encouragement and challenge for you. As you read each Scripture, sim-

ply listen to the voice of God speaking into your life personally.

3. **Reflection.** My heart in this section is not to take the place of God's voice but simply to make it personal, helping you practically apply any concept, thought, and necessary next step for you to take toward becoming more devout in your doubt.

4. **Prayer.** I believe prayer is our primary way of talking to God. If Scripture is God conversing with us, then we should definitely engage in the conversation. Through prayer, we have the great privilege to simply commune and communicate with the Creator of the heavens and the Earth, and while I offer a prayer to guide you in your conversation with God, please use it more as a launching pad to get your own conversation started.

Journal entry for July 20, 2020.

When you're just finding out.

Good day, friends. It's been a journey this past week. That is *the* understatement for the year. On Saturday, my wife Becky took me to the ER in what we thought would probably be a simple solution to a pretty good pain in the abdomen. Twenty-four hours later, we have doctors telling us it's cancer. What!!?? Never in a million years would we have thought that. So here we are a week later. Quarantined because of COVID-19 and on chemo (2nd day) because of cancer. 2020! What a year, huh?

So, what can I say to you? I need our faith family to understand something about my wife and me. Ten years ago, a similar medical issue happened, and we were spiritually unprepared for it. We panicked. I was frustrated with God. In my subtle arrogance, I thought, *How could God allow this to happen?* And while I didn't ever utter those words, in the core of my pride, I had the thought: *After all that I have done for Him, how could he!?* I'm even a bit embarrassed to write those words.

But this year is a new year. God has brought us a long way, and here we are, staring at cancer. This was certainly a surprise to discover this physical setback, but hear me on this new reality: **We may have been surprised, but we are not unprepared this time**. Now, my question is this: *So God, you allowed this to happen. What do you need from me in this season? How can I grow through this? How can I be used in the lives of my family, my church, this hospital floor?*

Don't hear what I'm not saying. I'm still nervous. I still get anxious. I still cry—as anyone would and has around the topic of cancer. I'm still frustrated that I cannot see my wife or my kids because of this stupid COVID virus. I'm still working through all of this with God. I'm just saying that I am confident that God's presence is here with me, in me, and working through me. No doubt in my mind. And despite all of the setbacks, I'm ready, Lord. Use me!

Love you guys. Hope I can encourage YOU today. Thank you for the prayer and support!

Paul (and Becky)

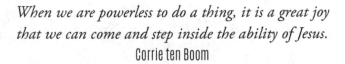

When we are powerless to do a thing, it is a great joy that we can come and step inside the ability of Jesus.
Corrie ten Boom

Scripture reading.

The eternal God is your refuge, and his everlasting arms are under you.

Deuteronomy 33:27a

Reflection.

Consider your own life and the surprises that have come your way. Be honest. What was your first response to God?

Prayer.

God, I don't understand why this is happening, but I understand that you want what's best for me. God, meet me in my doubt right now. Hold me up because I want to fall down. God, I need your presence now. Amen.

2

Journal Entry for July 22, 2020.

God's got this, I hope.

Greetings, friends. Thought I would give an update on my scene. Many have asked, so here we go . . .

On day four of chemotherapy. So far, thanks be to God, the effects have been mild. Just getting started so not entirely sure what is to come. I still have twenty-six treatments to go. But trusting in the same Spirit that raised Jesus from the dead to chase this cancer out of any potential grave. The topic of cancer and sickness isn't new to God. He's got this, I'm sure of it. I hope.

This is just the beginning of a five-month journey with the possibility of being home two to three weeks in the next five months. Hopefully, it will not take that long, but that is the plan at this point. So I'm still working on my responsibilities at the church, meeting with staff, and doing what I can. Much of the day today is turned over to some fantastic pastors and directors. I'm grateful for these beautiful people I get to lead and work with.

Many have asked how Becky and the kids are doing. They are well as can be. All of the kids will be coming to town the week I am home to rest. Looking forward to that as a couple of them are in different corners of the US. For now, it's all FaceTime as much as we can (picture below). Thank God for the technology that we have today. It's been a blessing.

And thank God for all of you and your encouraging notes, cards, gift cards, and random expressions of love. We cannot exist outside the community of Christ. We need each other. We're better together. The Baldwin family is better because of YOU.

Love and miss you all. Peace.

Paul

I know God will not give me anything I can't handle. I just wish that He didn't trust me so much.
Mother Teresa

Scripture reading.

When doubt fills my mind, your comfort gives me renewed hope and cheer.
Psalm 94:19

Reflection.

If you are able, write down three blessings in your life despite the presence of your sickness.

Prayer.

God, thank you for the blessings that are present in my life. Even though my mind is caught up in my newfound sickness, I still thank you for what is good in my life. Amen.

$$3$$

Journal Entry for July 23, 2020.

Give us this day . . .

Update for today. Got some good news! No cancer in the bone marrow. That was a big concern, to be sure, and it appears that we are free from it in those areas. Still, an aggressive cancer where it *is* located but believing that our current pathway of treatment is a pathway to progress and total restoration.

Finished the first round of twenty-four-hour-a-day for five days of treatment. One down, five more to go between now and December. Praising God for the limited side effects this first time around. No guarantee that I will be free from the deeper and more disturbing side effects in the future, but ours is to simply say, "God, give us THIS day, our daily bread . . ." I may be shifting that slightly out of context, but the idea is to simply trust God for his provision TODAY and expect that he's got our TOMOR-

ROW. That's what Becky and I (and the kids) are putting our hope in.

May God add HIS grace to your life. And may you see that grace at work in your life in the various conversations, transactions, and responses that you encounter today.

Final, cool story. So grateful to our Kids' Director Kathy Sosa and her amazing husband, Michael. They gave me the coolest gift of coloring books, brainteasers, and an activity bag. The next day (before I had really even explored this gift), I met Devon-Shawn, a ten-year-old boy with leukemia. Hair was already gone. Clearly frightened and overwhelmed. I immediately knew that this gift that was intended for me was really intended for Devon, so I asked the nurse to take this gift to him and he LOVED IT! How cool is God that he would move on the hearts of our people on *my* behalf, knowing where the intended destination really was? That's the God we serve. So cool and encouraging. Devon's smile was big yesterday, I am told. Hoping to get to talk to him today, but if not, I love our church and how they love people they don't even know. Keep up the great work church. #GodsGotThis #HeWill-BuildHisChurch

Faith is taking the first step, even when you
don't see the whole staircase.
Dr. Martin Luther King, Jr.

Scripture reading.

He who did not spare his own son, but gave him up for all of us—how will he not also, along with him, graciously give us all things.

Romans 8:32 (NIV)

Reflection.

Do you find yourself worrying about tomorrow's needs? Think of a time where God provided in the most unexpected way. What can you ask him for today? Thank him for taking care of you in that way. Be specific.

Prayer.

God, thank you for providing for me when _____. God, I'm asking you to do it again in your own way. Meet my needs today as you see fit. Amen.

4

When we pray together.

Greetings from the sixth-floor hotel (I mean hospital) room of Baptist Kendall Regional. I'm on the sixth floor of the building called Hope. Literally, this building has the name Hope. That's got to mean something right? For better or worse, this has become my home away from home as I head into week three of treatment.

I wanted to keep this one brief and simply say "thank you" to all who have expressed your love to Becky and me and the kids. It's amazing how God works when he showers us with his grace and love. More often than not, he demonstrates his love for us through his community.

I've said before that we are a very private family and often like to keep our "stuff" to ourselves. However, we know what happens when God's people come together, stand together, and pray together. Throughout Scripture,

God's heart is continually moved by such momentum. We don't always understand how and why, but we know that when God's reputation is put up as the highest calling, He shows up and shows off simply to affirm our praise of Him.

That's what's happening in our lives because of you. The prayer. The gifts. The meals. Even the financial support. The encouraging texts, Instagram messages, and Facebook posts from all over the country, reaching back over thirty years of friendships and family. So many unique expressions of support and love. We are simply floored and undone with so much compassion and grace and love and support.

No real new updates today. In fact, a very rough night last night but feeling so much better today. All good in the "neighborhood" as they say. We're seeing more victories than defeats.

We love and thank you with all that we have.

Pastor Paul (and Becky)

To be a Christian without prayer is no more possible than to be alive without breathing.
Dr. Martin Luther King, Jr.

Scripture reading.
Seek the Lord and his strength; seek his presence continually!
(English Standard Version)

Reflection.

Is there someone you can reach out to right now in your family or your circle of friends? Ask them to pray for you. You don't even need to be specific. Just ask for prayer and let them work it out with God on your behalf.

Prayer.

God, thank you for prayer. Although I don't always understand how it works or how you work, I want to believe that there is power available in prayer so thank you for those people you have brought into my life to pray for me. Amen.

5

Journal Entry for July 27, 2020.

Trying to be real about what is real.

Hello, friends. Thank you so much for your faithfulness in praying for us in this season.

I'm not going to lie to you. It was a rough weekend, but it's all part of the process. Not fun but asking God to give strength and encouragement. I've recently rediscovered this reality again in the Bible: Scripture actually calls us to this ideal.

I've just started reading through James with an old high school buddy, a thirty-year friendship. Been interesting and frustrating and curious all the same. James says that we should consider it *joy* when we face trials. In short, trials give us an opportunity to persevere in the strength and power of God. It shapes us. It moves us toward the better and best version of who God is making us to be in Christ. Sounds good. Sounds super spiritual. It is, but it just stinks when you're in the middle of it. Just calling it how I'm feeling it. :-(

Still, regardless of how I'm feeling physically, the spiritual reality is no less a truth for me, for you, for us. Asking you to pray with Becky and me as we explore this reality in our own lives and context. It's real.

Sorry—wish my post was a bit more eloquent. Trying to be real about what is real in my life. Trying to be real about where we're at. We love you all.

Pastor Paul

In God, there is no such thing as a
hopeless situation.
Rhonda Byrne

Scripture reading.

Consider it pure joy, my brothers and sisters, whenever you face trials of many kinds, because you know that the testing of your faith produces perseverance. Let perseverance finish its work so that you may be mature and complete, not lacking anything.
James 1:2-4 (NIV)

Reflection.

How do you typically respond when you get hit with bad news? Your initial reaction usually reflects who you really are but also that you are human. You're not a bad person. You're just being real about what is real. Still, is there an opportunity for growth? How so? Write those thoughts down.

Prayer.

God, I want to be the better and best version of who you made me to be. Help me to not just go through this season but to grow through this season. Amen.

6

Journal Entry for July 29, 2020.

God's glory will be increased.

Good morning, friends. We are grateful and overwhelmed by so much love from so many friends and family now all over the world—from our church campus community in Saut D'Eau, Haiti to a convent in the country of Columbia expressing their love and support. It's amazing how loud God's reputation gets as his community gathers in prayer. I don't fully know how the supernatural healing power of God works, and I'm old enough to not even try to pretend to understand. I just know that as God's community participates in his divine nature, God's glory *will* be increased. And in his glory, there is divine healing. It's crazy to even try to comprehend. Thank you for participating on our behalf. We are humbled.

Update: Into week three now and still in the hospital. Better day today than the past few days. Hoping to be home next week, joining my children and Becky for some time of rest from this mess before coming back for round two of chemo. Still have several days of restoration getting blood counts to where they need to be before it's safe to go home. Praying that happens more quickly than normal.

———————————◼▢◼———————————

If you keep your eyes open enough, oh, the stuff you will learn, oh the most wonderful stuff!
Dr. Theodor Suess Geisel

Scripture reading.
So be truly glad. There is wonderful joy ahead, even though you must endure many trials for a little while. These trials will show that your faith is genuine. It is being tested as fire tests and purifies gold—though your faith is far more precious than mere gold. So, when your faith remains strong through many trials, it will bring you much praise and glory and honor on the day when Jesus Christ is revealed to the whole world.

1 Peter 1:6-7

Reflection.
Even though it's hard to conceive of in your current circumstances, how do you see God's reputation increasing even in the midst of your mess? Write down one or two thoughts.

Prayer.

God, increase my faith in this season. God show up and show off in my life and through my life today. I want your reputation to increase. Amen.

7

Journal Entry for July 31, 2020.

This is messy.

Greetings, friends. Thought I would share some technical stuff with you with an interesting spiritual twist at the end.

Rough night last night. Thought we were through the "messy" part of it. Had some radical pain all through my bones. Like, I could not sleep at all. The nurses gave me morphine, which honestly didn't help, even with a couple of other drugs. I have no clue what those were. They told me. I wasn't paying attention. Too much pain.

It turns out that pain in the bones is caused by the white blood cells contacting with and dying from the chemo, while at the same time, the new white cells they are injecting, to stimulate white blood cell regeneration, are growing. So bad cells out and good cells are regenerating, causing a contraction and expansion in the bones, in particular in the chest and shoulder areas along with the legs and lower back area—all the areas I where I had gnarly pain. Crazy. *Growing pains.*

It doesn't happen often but it does happen, and it usually happens at night, as it did with me. I'm better now. Sore . . . like the body has a hangover from all of the pain and the lack of sleep, but at least we have an answer that makes sense. It makes sense to me. So this may be the case for the next twenty-four to forty-eight hours, and if it is the case, they have Oxycodone (the good stuff) to help me sort through it and sleep. Other than that, my blood levels are rising, and they fully expect me to be home (as expected) by Monday for a week of rest before we begin again: cycle two.

Thought I would share some of the technical stuff for this reason:

As they explained things to me later, I was literally *amazed* at the human body and what it can tolerate (like chemo . . . the bad stuff) and *how the human body is designed to reiterate goodness, even when bad things happen to it.*

That is ALL God.

That God would create a human body that is designed to *live* and *flourish* despite the bad things that do happen. When toxic pollution comes into the body, God designed the body to expel that which is not from him. Man, you could take this illustration in so many directions. Maybe

I will someday when I'm back on that platform preaching to you all.

For now, I'm just celebrating a God who has got this! #GodsGotThis!

Psalm 139. He knows everything about me. He knows my thoughts, how many hairs I have on my head, and how many white blood cells need to be made up to make me healthy again. Just gotta trust his next move.

But first, I'm going to take a long nap.

I have held many things in my hands, and I have lost them all. But whatever I have placed in God's hands, that I still possess.
Corrie ten Boom

Scripture reading.
You made all the delicate, inner parts of my body
and knit me together in my mother's womb.
Thank you for making me so wonderfully complex!
Your workmanship is marvelous—how well I know it.
You watched me as I was being formed in utter seclusion,
as I was woven together in the dark of the womb.
You saw me before I was born.
Every day of my life was recorded in your book.
Every moment was laid out
before a single day had passed.

How precious are your thoughts about me, O God.
They cannot be numbered!
I can't even count them;
they outnumber the grains of sand!
And when I wake up,
you are still with me!

Psalm 139: 13-18

Reflection.

Consider your own life and the surprises that have come your way. Be honest; what was your first response to God?

Prayer.

God, thank you for making me so wonderfully complex! I surrender my physical body back over to you. Thank you that you are with me. Amen.

(8)

This is real, and this is uncertain.

Hey, friends. It's Sunday, August 2nd. Hoping today is the last day in the hospital for cycle one. Kids are coming home, and we'll get this next week to spend together before I come back for cycle two (2nd of six cycles).

We *did* hear back from the cellular study on the initial biopsy on this tumor. We learned that of the non-Hodgkin's lymphomas, there are basically three levels of aggression, we'll call them small, medium, and large (they have way more scientific terms) in both their aggressive nature and treatment.

I have the medium level.

So the good news is that the treatment (and effects) should not get any worse, theoretically. The challenging news is that it's all still uncertain. We have a plan. The plan

29

seems to be going as planned. It's just real and uncertain as these things often are. **As you pray, please pray that the LOVE of God will continue to push through and eclipse the FEAR that emerges from time to time.** The fear is there, to be sure. But again, God has done a beautiful job (as he often does) of making sure that his love is consistently greater than that fear. He has demonstrated that love in so many ways, including his loving community (that's ya'll, folks). Grateful for that.

Outside of that, I'm very much looking forward to the break with my family. Just want to get lost in that time with them. Love you all and appreciate you all so much.

Peace and love to you.

Paul

I firmly believe that in every situation, no matter how difficult, God extends grace greater than the hardship, and strength and peace of mind that can lead us to a place higher than we were before.
Andy Griffith

Scripture reading.

For the Spirit God gave us does not make us timid, but gives us power, love and self-discipline.
1 Timothy 1:7 (NIV)

Reflection.

Be honest; your fear is real. So is your faith. Oftentimes, fear and faith co-exist. Sometimes, your fear eclipses faith. The Scripture promises that the Spirit of God can push out the fear we experience.

Write down three things you are afraid of right now. Then, right next to those fears, write things you believe God can do about those fears.

Prayer.

God, please give me more faith over my fear today. God, I know that you are bigger than these fears, so I choose to give you the pressure in exchange for your peace. Amen.

Journal Entry for August 5, 2020.

Hope for the best; prepare for the worst?

Good morning, friends. I want to provide an update. Home this week with family. It's been a sweet time of reunion, eating, watching movies, and simply relaxing. That was what the doctor ordered, so I am gladly obeying.

I woke up a bit earlier than the rest of my family today, so I thought I would share my morning word from God. Each morning, while home, I've woken up with my head in very different places—sometimes positive and sometimes not so positive.

This morning, I was thinking about this phrase, **"Hope for the best; prepare for the worst."** Ever heard it? I understand the concept behind it, but in the Kingdom of God, I wonder if that is a phrase that we should use? I mean, I don't want to overthink it, and honestly, I'll probably continue to use this phrase but push back with me for a moment.

What if, from Heaven's perspective, our call is to "hope for the best *and* prepare for the best" in all seasons? In other words, what if we knew, in faith, without a shadow of a doubt, the best was yet to come and our call is to live in that reality?

My wife once wrote, "**faith really isn't faith until it's all you have left to hang onto.**" She wrote that phrase nearly twenty years ago, and it's never left me. Or has it? Perhaps, it's just a phrase that's in my head but hasn't really dropped to my heart pumping blood to the rest of my body for action. Maybe it does some days and not on other days. Maybe I'm overthinking it. I'm probably overthinking it. Perhaps, I'm being too hard on myself.

Like Peter, walking on the water with his eyes on Jesus (Matthew 14), *I want to walk today with my eyes on Jesus, hoping and expecting and preparing as if all of the resources of Heaven are on my side.* Like Peter, I'm sure fear will try to punch holes in my faith, but when that happens, I'll look to Jesus, again and again, to reach his hand out to pull me closer to him. That is my prayer for me, my family, and for you all.

Update.

I've got a *big* appointment today to walk through the course of treatment for the next five months. A bit nervous but hoping and preparing for the *best* because the *best* is yet to come!

Love you guys.
Paul and Becky.

Although the threads of my life have often seemed knotted, I know, by faith, that on the other side of the embroidery, there is a crown.
Corrie ten Boom

Scripture reading.

Now faith is the substance of things hoped for, the evidence of things not seen.
Hebrews 11:1 (KJV)

Reflection.

Faith is more than just believing. It's living in a way that shows that you trust in God, regardless of what comes your way. That's easier said than done, to be sure. That's why we need outside help. That is where God's grace comes in. God's grace is God's presence, power, and provision motivated by God's love for you.

Where do you need God's presence, power, and provision today?

Prayer.

God, I want to walk today with my eyes on Jesus, hoping and expecting and preparing as if all of the

*resources of Heaven are on my side. God, give me the
faith to live in that way today. Amen.*

Journal Entry for August 9, 2020.

Life and uncertainty.

Good Sunday to you. It's been a few days since I last checked in with you all. I received several texts and phone calls asking for an update. Thank you for being interested. Here is the update.

Great week this past week with Becky and the three younger kiddos (picture below). So sweet and refreshing to enjoy the "normal" things, apart from the reality of cancer and the underlying uncertainty of it all. I'm sure you have something in your life that is uncertain, albeit big or small, unresolved, or still needing answers to questions you have. Despite the reality of illness still being present, it was nice to break from it all, even if in only in my mind. :-)

I've been thinking a lot this week about life and uncertainty and questions that I hope to have answered in these next few weeks. Here is what God has been showing me the last couple of days.

The truth is that I am not my own and neither are you. *1 Corinthians 6:19–20 reminds us that we are no longer our own, we belong to Jesus and have given him full authority over everything—the spiritual things to be sure—but also the physical shells of our bodies, regardless of the condition that our physical bodies are in.*

You know that is what happens when we give our lives, fully surrendered, to God. We exchange our stuff for God's stuff. We exchange our messes for God's blessings. We exchange the pressure of the world with the provisions of Heaven. The problem is that when life goes south, gets uncertain, perhaps bends a bit sideways, we want to take control of what we have "left" and try to make sense of it all.

We ask questions like *God, why is this happening to me?* or *God, when will I get through this?* or we even begin making promises like *God, if I can make it through this, I will . . .* It's just the way we are as human beings. We like to bargain with God.

I love how Dallas Willard delineates between my life and Jesus's life lived through me. There is a difference. In *The Great Omission: Reclaiming Jesus's Essential Teachings on Discipleship,* he says, "The problem comes when we mistake the vessel for the treasure, for the treasure is the life and power of Jesus Christ."

I have to remember that my life is not really my own. I cannot be confused about what is really important. **It's the life of Jesus in me and through me as long as I'm**

breathing. *That's all that matters.* Everything that happens to me, through me, and because of me, regardless if God causes it or allows it, *should reflect the matchless grace and love and power of Jesus.* That is my prayer for the good days and the not-so-great days ahead. That is my prayer for you, as well, this week. May it be so, in Jesus's name, amen.

Update:

I'm back in the hospital for round two of chemo. This is the week that should get kind of hairy and messy. Not looking forward to it. Please pray for strength and endurance for me. Please pray for Becky and the kids as they are home making things happen there.

Love you all.

Paul

The problem comes when we mistake the vessel for the treasure, for the treasure is the life and power of Jesus Christ.
Dallas Willard

Scripture reading.

Do you not know that your bodies are temples of the Holy Spirit, who is in you, whom you have received from God? You are not your own; you were bought at a price. Therefore, honor God with your bodies.

1 Corinthians 6:19-20 (NIV)

Reflection.

Perhaps what is happening to you physically is exhausting you emotionally. It's too heavy to carry. Make a small list of the "baggage" you would like to drop off to God for him to carry. Perhaps it's emotional baggage, physical baggage, or even relational baggage. Write that list down on a piece of paper.

Take that piece of paper, crunch it up with your hand, and then toss it in the trash as a symbol that you are surrendering this "baggage" to God today. As you do, pray this prayer below:

Prayer.

God, at this moment, I surrender my physical body, my emotions, my frustrations, and my disappointment. I surrender it all to you and ask that you give me all that you have in exchange. I need your peace right now. Amen.

Journal Entry for August 13, 2020.

No desire.

Good morning, friends! Day 4 of round two of chemo. Tough day yesterday. Interesting day, in that the day started beautifully with me feeling like I was sailing through this round of chemo. Then WHAM, the day took a turn downward and left me feeling miserable, not wanting to eat, walk, or even think.

It's so frustrating that a situation can turn so quickly.

I just wanted to do nothing, which is the worst thing you can do while on chemo. The experts around here say you're supposed to eat, walk, drink water, and stay out of bed during treatment.

I gotta be honest. I didn't want to do any of that.

The things that were recommended I do to thrive during treatment, I didn't do. I just wanted to survive. That's probably a dramatic portrayal of my day—but not too far off. When you're in the middle of the mess, you don't always think straight do you?

Such a defeating feeling. Just wanted to quit and walk out.

Even so, about halfway through my day, I realized that I needed to do something to contribute to my well-being. I got a text from Becky asking me if I had eaten. I had, sort of, but hadn't done much more of what was instructed. The doctors were doing all that they were supposed to do. The nurses were doing their homework. Even the custodians and catering crew came on schedule to clean my room and drop off food.

Everyone was doing their part, but for a few hours, I was not.

Is that okay?

The answer is honestly and probably "yes" and "no."

The common phrase around here is that you should listen to your body and do what your body tells you to do. And while I agree with that idea (and eventually complied), *I think, sometimes, we can deceive ourselves into thinking we should be doing something we really shouldn't be doing.* So I rested because I needed to rest. And that's okay. But then something switched in my head, something that also compelled me to eat, to walk, and to drink water. Perhaps it was the text from Becky. I don't know. *Either way, it's what I needed to do to participate toward thriving over surviving.* I honestly didn't want to do it and didn't enjoy doing it. **I just trusted the prescription of the experts**

who had laid out an obviously proven pathway for success: cancer survival.

They have been down this road. I have not. They must know best, right?

Long messy story short, we ended the evening on a "win," feeling better around midnight. Exhausted, yes. However, as they promised, I did make it over that downturn and feel great this morning.

Here's to obedience!

It isn't always pretty but it's the best pathway to walk.

Perhaps, from my reflection, there is a *bigger* something to learn about life and faith for all of us. I won't do that for you today. Praying the Holy Spirit does that for you at some point today or this week. I *will* leave you with this Scripture as a prompt and then thank you all again for your continued support, love, and prayer for me and my family.

Love and miss you guys.

Here's to thriving over surviving!

Peace and love to you as you persevere in your own journey.

Pablo.

God doesn't require us to succeed;
he only requires that you try.
Mother Teresa

Scripture reading.

For this very reason, make every effort to add to your faith goodness; and to goodness, knowledge; and to knowledge, self-control; and to self-control, perseverance; and to perseverance, godliness; and to godliness, mutual affection; and to mutual affection, love.

2 Peter 1:5-7

Reflection.

Take a break from being you for a moment. Put yourself in the position of the person taking care of you. What would you say to you? How would you instruct *you*? What prescription would you offer? Now, jump back into yourself again. What does obedience look like in this season for you?

Prayer.

God, help me lean on you at this moment. You know I don't want to but I know I need to. God, help me to see that you know what is best for me and help me to trust you to get me through what I'm going through. Amen.

$$\text{(12)}$$

Journal Entry for August 16, 2020.

Hungry for peace.

Good morning, friends. Update: Rough night last night. Ugh! I won't bore you with the gruesome details. It just is what it is. :-(

Interesting night in the process where you just kind of have to deal with what the reality of the side effects of chemotherapy. No way around it other than tolerating it and maybe getting some drugs to help you through it. Funny, *not* funny experience.

What is wild is that on and off all evening, I had two Scriptures in my mind: Job 3:26 and Isaiah 6:23. These two Scriptures were almost at war with each other, you could say.

Job 3:26.

> *I have no peace, no quietness. I have no rest; only trouble comes.*

and . . .

Isaiah 6:23.

> *You will keep him in perfect peace, Whose mind is stayed on You, Because he trusts in You.*

Now, I don't even want to pretend to compare my life to the life of Job and what loss he experienced. His story is almost unfathomable to me. But I can say again, for any of us, that all pain and suffering is real and can steal our peace, even for moments at a time. The promise is that in these moments, we reach for a peace that is "other than" what is possible in the natural. When we are desperate to breathe, our focus on air becomes radically acute and focused, doesn't it? We think about nothing else.

Easier said than done, to be sure, but what other options do we have? All other options fail us.

I've been walking with Jesus for almost thirty-five years now, and I haven't found any other source for long-lasting peace. Praying *you* find this same peace that goes beyond all understanding in whatever pathway you're walking today.

Philippians 4:7.

Love and miss you all.
Paul

God longs to quiet your heart with his love, to calm your fears, insecurities, and doubts with his presence.
Renee Swope

Scripture reading.

Don't worry about anything; instead, pray about everything. Tell God what you need, and thank him for all he has done. Then you will experience God's peace, which exceeds anything we can understand. His peace will guard your hearts and minds as you live in Christ Jesus.
Philippians 4:6-7

Reflection.

There is a difference between worry and concern. Worry sees the obstacle as real and blocking *my* limited peace. Concern sees the obstacle as real but as an opportunity to give it to God in exchange for *his* unlimited peace. Write down your main worry today. This is what you need God to help you lay down.

Prayer.

God, I need your peace right now. My peace is limited. Your peace is unlimited. Help me to lay down whatever obstacle is in my life right now and pick up your peace. Amen.

(13)

Journal Entry for August 17, 2020.

I'm still smiling.

Good day friends. BTW . . . I'm still smiling just in case you were wondering! ;-)

Going to keep this one short. *It was a good day.* Blood counts are where they need to be. No side effects outside of a sore throat, which is normal after chemo. I can handle that. From the oncologist's perspective, I'm on track this week and where I need to be. That's good news.

It's nice to have a bit of space to breathe and take in the goodness of God *while* feeling good. You've heard me say that we need to praise God in the valley. That is where we find real sticky and practical peace. *Today, it's important to remember to thank God for his goodness, even when the pressure is not so heavy.*

So to that end, I'll offer one of my favorite Psalms in hopes that you will join me in your own brief praise-break . . . wherever you are.

Peace and love to you guys. Thanks for standing with my family.

God has infinite attention to spare for each one of us. You're as much alone with Him as if you were the only being he had ever created.
C.S. Lewis

Scripture reading.
A David Psalm

I bless God every chance I get;
my lungs expand with his praise.
I live and breathe God;
if things aren't going well, hear this and be happy:
Join me in spreading the news;
together let's get the word out.
God met me more than halfway,
he freed me from my anxious fears.
Look at him; give him your warmest smile.
Never hide your feelings from him.
When I was desperate, I called out,
and God got me out of a tight spot.
God's angel sets up a circle

of protection around us while we pray.
Open your mouth and taste, open your eyes and see—
how good God is.
Blessed are you who run to him.
Worship God if you want the best;
worship opens doors to all his goodness.

Psalm 34

Reflection.

There is an old phrase that says we should stop and smell the roses. Despite all that you could justifiably complain about, what can you thank God for right now? Write two or three thankful thoughts down.

Prayer.

God, as I look at my 'thankful' list right now, THANK YOU for the smaller blessings in my life. Thank you for never abandoning me. Amen.

14

Journal Entry for August 18, 2020.

Worship.

For those of you who are wrestling in a battle of some kind. Take a few minutes, quiet yourself, and listen to a special YouTube video. Search for "Never Lost" featuring Israel Houghton | Live From Elevation Ballantyne | Elevation Worship.

Practice worship over worry.

Love you guys.

Paul

———————————■ ⊢ ■———————————

The more you pray, the less you'll panic. The more you worship, the less you worry. You'll feel more patient and less pressured.
Rick Warren

Scripture reading.

Give all your worries and cares to God, for he cares about you.

1 Peter 5:7

Reflection.

They say that worship is the antidote for worry. Consider those areas of worry in your life right now as if you were putting them into your hands. Hold them for a moment. Listen to the song in the YouTube link, if you haven't already. Read the Scripture below, and at some point during the song, simply raise your hands to Heaven, as if symbolically releasing those worries to God.

Prayer.

God, thank you for caring for me. Thank you for taking my worry. Help me to release my worry in times of worship. Amen.

15

Journal Entry for August 20, 2020.

Going home.

I'm literally heading home right from the hospital. I will be home for a week.

Gratitude is the ability to experience life as a gift. It liberates us from the prison of self-preoccupation.
John Ortberg

Scripture reading.

Rejoice always, pray continually, give thanks in all circumstances; for this is God's will for you in Christ Jesus.

1 Thessalonians 5:16-18 (NIV)

Reflection.

I know, this was the only thing I had written on this day. Seems weird and perhaps even a bit rude to include it. However, I promised that I would share my entire journey, and this letter was part of it. It may even frustrate you because perhaps you can't go home right now; you're not feeling better in this moment, or you're still stuck and it's frustrating.

This is precisely why I left this entry in here. A huge component of learning to be devout in our doubt is practicing gratefulness to God for the progress of others, even when your own progress is lagging.

Prayer.

God, help me be grateful for what you are doing in other people's lives. I want to be that person who celebrates with others, regardless of my own setbacks. Amen.

16

Journal Entry for August 26, 2020.

What if?

Greetings, friends. Thought I would touch base and get you an update. I'm currently home for a week, trying to recoup and catch a breath. Been a rough weekend, but yesterday and today have been much better. I gotta be honest when I say that the physical up and down is emotionally exhausting. Still, we live day-by-day, placing our hand in the hand of a God who controls all things. There's just no other way to walk well in life but to stay close to God, no matter what.

I actually just got off the phone with a bro in my small group. It was kind of both a business call and a personal call, but the call was life-giving for sure. At the end of the call, he simply took off the "work" hat and asked to pray for me. *As the Holy Spirit often does in our time of need, knowing what we need prayer for even when we don't know*

*how to pray, my buddy began to pray over the "what ifs" in
my life.*

PAUSE. Consider the "what ifs" in your own life.

What if I can just close this deal? What if I were
twenty pounds lighter? What if my kid would make better choices? What if I hadn't said that, done that, thought
that? What if I made $50K more a year? *What if the cancer
doesn't get cleaned up and cleared out?*

What if? What if? What if? Would you agree that the
question of "what if" could certainly catapult us into a
place of *hope* or *hopelessness*, depending on the day? A very
vulnerable place to be sure. An emotionally exhausting
place that many of us have been, I'm sure.

Not even knowing where my head fully was, my buddy
just simply prayed and allowed the Holy Spirit to use him
as a conduit for breathing life into another brother (that's
me). He just prayed as he felt led, and God showed up
and showed off in my heart at that moment. So good. So
simple So needed. *Such* a different posture I had after the
call than before the call.

Listen, I don't know where you are at with your own
head space. I don't know what is going on in your life this
week. I *am* praying that you will either be the receiver
of encouragement or be the encourager today. Heck, I
hope and pray BOTH happen in your life today. This is
how God's people roll. Give yourself over to it. The better
and best version of who you were created to be is on the
other side of that discipline.

Therefore encourage one another and build each other up, just as in fact you are doing (1 Thessalonians 5:11). Thanks for faithfully serving our family in prayer/care/compassion. I wish I could better articulate in words how grateful we are to you all.

Peace and love to you guys.

Paul

Sometimes when we get overwhelmed,
we forget how big God is.
A.W. Tozer

Scripture reading.

Therefore encourage one another and build each other up, just as in fact you are doing.
1 Thessalonians 5:11.

Reflection.

Consider the "what if" scenarios you've played out in your head, even this past week. Do those scenarios generate hope or hopelessness as you think of them? Now, consider the people who speak into your life on a regular basis. Do those people bring hope or hopelessness? Make sure you are seeking out people who add hope to your life.

Prayer.

God, thank you for working through people in my life. Thank you for encouraging me through these friends in the "what if" scenarios of my life. Help me to be an encouragement to all of those around me. God, only you can do this in and through me. Make it so, in Jesus's name. Amen.

17

Journal Entry for August 29, 2020.

Feeling like I'm falling apart.

Hello, friends. Dropping in to update you. I'm still at home. Got some good news and challenging news.

The good news.

Don't have to go back to the hospital immediately. After having completed rounds one and two of chemo, the doctors feel we have made enough progress and improvement that I can do rounds three through six as an outpatient during the day, sleeping at home during the evening. *What do I mean by improvement?* That means that the area of focus (the malignant and ulcerative tumor) has decreased significantly in size. Additionally, the area in question is not vulnerable to perforation to the rest of the bowels. In short, that's good news. That's progress. Praising God for that good news!

The challenging news.

This week has been *super* rough and inconsistent with respect to my health. Constantly nauseous and feeling super frail with almost zero energy. This particular week in the cycle is typically strong going into the week I would start chemo. Ugh. Frustrating and defeating. I feel like I'm falling apart.

Still, I'm asking for God's encouragement to do just what he promised to do—give courage in times like these. This is, after all, what the word "encouragement" literally points to in Scripture. *Such strength comes from no other place in my experience. I have found that true healing—be it emotional, spiritual, and even physical in some cases—begins when we place our full surrender in the great physician trusting him to provide the heavenly resources we need to literally live another day.* This practice has been tough for me this week. Still, I'm *leaning* in this direction.

Asking you to pray specifically this quote (below) over me. I'll return the favor and pray the same for you. Deal?

Peace and love to you guys.

Paul

———————————◼☐◼———————————

> *Healing begins when, in the face of our own darkness, we recognize our helplessness and surrender our need for control . . . we face what is, and we ask for mercy.*
> Henri Nouwen

Scripture reading.

If your heart is broken, you'll find God right there; if you're kicked in the gut, he'll help you catch your breath.

Psalm 34:18 (The Message)

Reflection.

When you lay in bed at night, and there is nothing left to think about, what do you think about? Write that thought down. Chances are that it is this thought that has control over you. This is the area to surrender to God today. Give yourself the gift of living in freedom. God wants to carry this burden for you so that you can be the better (and best) version of humanity that he intended you to be.

Prayer.

God, I need you at this moment right now. What I have is not enough to bring peace. I need what only you can bring. Do in me what only you can do. Show up and show off in my life today. Amen.

18

Journal Entry for September 4, 2020.

Suffering.

September 4th: Our 27th wedding anniversary is today. Going to spend the day in the hospital for the fifth and final day of chemo, round three this week. Three more rounds to go after this. The fifth day is always an intense treatment—call it shock chemo (for lack of a better description) to finish out the cycle. This will be the first time I do it in the hospital and immediately come home for recovery. Not going to lie. I'm kind of nervous about the recovery time at home away from the "comfort" and security of the nurses and hospital staff who have been close by. Please pray all goes according to the best of plans this weekend, as these next few days are typically when I am most vulnerable to sickness and side effects. Usually not fun at all.

A friend of mine (Nik Korba . . . for those who know and love him) recently shared this beautiful quote with me from the novel *The Song of the Lark* by Willa Cather:

> *Something pulled in her—and broke. . . . But when the sun rose in the morning, she was far away. It was all behind her, and she knew that she would never cry like that again. People live through such pain only once; pain comes again, but it finds a tougher surface.*

I recently shared with one of my daughters that suffering is a common place where spiritual awakening happens. It's when we're most vulnerable and, therefore, most ready to receive help from outside of ourselves. It's the craziest thing.

As an example, I can remember very difficult evenings out at sea, working the tug boats in the Pacific Ocean. It was always a welcoming experience when the morning would emerge, and the turbulent sea would inevitably get calmer—how beautiful the sun was breaking through the darkness almost immediately eliminating the rowdy night of work and fear and danger that was usually present in the kind of work we did. On our way back to port, "it was all behind" us, and the safety and security of "home" were imminent, to be sure.

I love this quote by Willa Cather. Reminds me of the "home base" that we find in the presence and power of Jesus who *is* the *pioneer* of faith. That is, he has gone before us in suffering and has gone before us in victory. He is the reason we can find "home" in times of suffering. *He has experienced every kind of suffering that many of us can only imagine.*

Jesus has also experienced the glory and home of Heaven that none of us have yet to experience in its fullness. When times get dark. When the situation is fragile and uncertain, we can fix our eyes on him and find any kind of peace when the immediate is uncertain.

I pray for you often in whatever tough situation you find yourself in today. Thank you for praying for me. Thank you for praying this reality over us, our family. Someday, this will all be behind us, and we'll never cry again. For now, we live with the peace that we are being perfected in faith. Amen.

It takes courage to live through suffering,
and it takes honesty to observe it.
C.S. Lewis

Scripture reading.
Therefore, since we are surrounded by such a great cloud of witnesses, let us throw off everything that hinders and the sin that so easily entangles. And let us run with perseverance the race marked out for us, fixing our eyes on Jesus, the pioneer and perfecter of faith. For the joy set before him he endured the cross,

scorning its shame, and sat down at the right hand of the throne of God.

Hebrews 11:1-2

Reflection.

There is usually a connection within a community of people who have similar experiences, whether it be a celebration, common activity, or yes, a common hurt, pain, or suffering. Is it comforting to know that within that community, we have a God-man who can identify with our experience? Not only that, Jesus can and is willing to lead us through such experiences with his grace, his comfort, and his encouragement. Why not reach out to him right now using the prayer below as a guide?

Prayer.

Jesus, I thank you for meeting me in this season of suffering. I'm grateful that you can identify with me, knowing what I'm going through. Give me what I need today, not just for my sake but for the sake of someone else. Amen.

19

Journal Entry for September 8, 2020.

More suffering.

Good morning, friends. Thought I would offer an update within what we're calling the "tough week."

Recall how my particular regiment has been playing out:

- Week 1 - chemo
- Week 2 - side effects/tough week
- Week 3 - bounce back/strong week of recouping.

So I'm not sleeping well. Vivid dreams. Super sore throat. Body aches. Dizzy. Feeling very fragile. Uninterested in drinking water, even though I know I need to stay hydrated. No nausea so far this time around—praise God. Just not the best week so far. All good.

Day by day, they say. ;-)

Not sure if this is going to sound morbid or not, but I'll go ahead put it out there. *Been thinking a lot about suffering lately* and how necessary it is to truly experience life in its fullness as Jesus describes in John 10:10.

The basic idea is this: **You cannot fully appreciate the light until you've sat in the darkness a bit.**

C.S. Lewis writes again about suffering. "Try to exclude the possibility of suffering which the order of nature and the existence of free wills involved, and you find that you have excluded life itself." Think about any season of growth you've experienced. It probably involved suffering. Suffering is a part of life and positions us, humbles us, even humiliates us to a place of admission that we cannot do it by ourselves. In essence, we are knocked down to a place of full surrender to something greater than ourselves that wants to rescue and restore us to the better and best versions of ourselves. In those seasons, we say, "Wow, that was a tough season, we learned so much, we grew so much!"

In that same season, a deeper community was formed, character grew exponentially, maturity flowered. **We grew up in that season, even if just a bit more.**

The way of Jesus involves both *glory* and *suffering*. Look at his own earthy life for proof of that reality. If I'm truly walking in the way of Jesus, it's hard to avoid the reality that both suffering and glory are necessary for our faith walks. We don't desire to suffer. We don't invite suffering in. Just don't be too quick to dismiss suffering in your own life. It could be that the better version of who you are is on the other side of suffering. Not sure what path you're on today and not sure where this connects with you.

Praying God gives you the faith to keep going.

Paul

We are not necessarily doubting that God will do the best for us; we are wondering how painful the best will turn out to be.
C.S. Lewis

Scripture reading.

For this light momentary affliction is preparing for us an eternal weight of glory beyond all comparison, as we look not to the things that are seen but to the things that are unseen. For the things that are seen are transient, but the things that are unseen are eternal.

2 Corinthians 4:17-18 (ESV)

Reflection.

The idea that suffering is an important part of our maturation process is surely quite morbid but consider this reality for a moment. It's not that we go looking for it. Just don't ignore the potential growth opportunity within suffering. Consider this question whenever you experience suffering: "Will I simply go through this season, or will I grow through this season?" How you answer this question could change the trajectory of your life.

Prayer.

God, I don't just want to go through this season. I want to grow through this season. I don't want to be bitter. I want to be better. Give me the strength and wisdom to lean in that direction. Amen.

20

How grace works.

Happy Monday to you all.

Welcome to the "strong week."

What does the "strong week" mean again? It means that within the three-week cycle of chemo, this is the week where white blood cell counts are where they need to be, hemoglobin is where it needs to be, chemo has dissipated a bit, allowing the body to bounce back and be what it's supposed to be for a week, more or less. The STRONG WEEK! Hooray~

Next week, we'll start all over with round four of chemo. Ugh. For now, we'll enjoy the STRONG week!

So while I was on a walk yesterday, it occurred to me why the strong week is the strong week. What I said above. *Everything in me is where it needs to be the way it was*

75

intended to be, more or less. Then, I began thinking about my own faith walk and the seasons where I have been weak. What was missing? I also began to take inventory of my stronger faith seasons. What was present?

As I walked yesterday listening to some worship music, breathing in the fresh air, enjoying the 82-degree, non-humid South Florida air, *I realized the answer to both questions above is in God's grace.* The reality is that God's grace is available to you and me 24/7. He's willing to give it. Grace. What we have denied as unmerited favor with God. Or, in other words, God loves us not because of anything we've done but because we are his, and he just wants to love us.

In fact, Scripture says that he's willing to "lavish" it (love) on us. John (in the ancient Scriptures) writes, "How great is the Father's love that he *lavished* on us. that we should be called sons and daughters of God! And that is what we are! (italics mine)" (1 John 3:1).

The word *lavish* literally means to give something in great, generous, and extravagant amounts. **This is what God wants to do for you and me!** The problem is that we don't always receive it for various reasons. We put up roadblocks to his grace. We look to other sources of supply for our strength. We find greater value elsewhere other than what God offers. We all do this. It's a part of our human condition.

Maybe I'm goofy, but this is what I think about when I think about white and red blood cells being where they need to be and doing what they need to do. *Spiritually, I need the grace of God to be present doing its job making me into the person I was meant to be.* Praying that over me and over you today.

Hope that my journey encourages your journey today. I'm humbled that you would even take the time to read this. **And THANK YOU, THANK YOU, THAN YOU** for praying for me, Becky, and the kiddos. This divine community means more than you will probably ever know. *You* are part of the grace God is lavishing on us!

Grateful.

Paul

I do not understand the mystery of grace,
only that it meets us where we are but does not
leave us where it found us.
Anne Lamott

Scripture reading.

How great is the Father's love that he lavished on us. that we should be called sons and daughters of God! And that is what we are!
1 John 3:1

For in him we live, and move, and have our being; as certain also of your own poets have said, for we are also his offspring.
Acts 17:28 (NKJV)

Reflection.

Read the two Scripture verses once more. What are the first words that come to your mind as you read these verses? Write those thoughts down. If you knew, without a shadow of a doubt, that God was ready to "lavish" grace on you today, how would that impact your thought process right now?

Prayer.

God, I'm ready and willing to receive whatever you want to give me today. Fill me up with your grace. Amen.

Journal Entry for September 21, 2020.

The end of myself.

Good day to you. Thank you for faithfully standing with Becky and me during this crazy and uncertain season.

So I was reflecting this morning a bit on my high school sporting experience. Tell you why in just thirty seconds. Back in "the day," I was a 260-pound defensive tackle at Morro Bay High School. Our football team was not so great, only winning a very few games . . . very few. Like, we were terrible! However, I was also part of the track team, coached by Carey Narreli. This guy was a winning coach coaching both girls' varsity basketball and the track team. Both teams experienced a great deal of success each year under the leadership and inspiration of Coach Narreli.

Coach Narreli had a way of pushing you beyond what you could handle. If I thought I only had two miles in me, Coach had a way of getting more, pushing me to run that extra mile. I can remember one example where Coach gave his normal routine, running the beach to Morro Rock (a local natural landmark) and back. Usually, we would jump into workouts after that particular "warm-up." Not this time. As we approached the school, we heard Coach Narreli yelling, *"Keeping running, let's knock out one more mile!"* and sending us to the field surrounded by a quarter-mile track. I was spent. I was exhausted. I had nothing left in me. In my mind, there was no way I could run one more mile but somehow did.

Ever been pushed beyond what you thought you could handle? Yeah, me too! Honestly, I'm exhausted and spent even as I type this. *Today I start round four of chemotherapy, and there is not a whisper of excitement in me over it.* I'm literally DONE with this process. I get that it needs to happen. I get that it's a process that is not only going to make me physically better, it's also making me mentally and spiritually stronger. I get it. But today, I'm done. I cannot run one more metaphorical mile.

Here is the word that God has given me this weekend. *We don't typically find out what God can really do in us until we run out of our own resources.* I've lived enough life to experience this spiritual reality.

Paul the Apostle promises this reality in Philippians 4:13, where he offers a promise that we can do all things through Jesus, who is the true source and supply of the strength that we need, regardless of context or circumstance. **When you've come to the end of yourself, that is where you usually find Jesus, and all of the**

resources of Heaven, waiting for you. This is *the* promise for me and you this morning. This is what I'm claiming today. I'm asking God to supply what I cannot give myself. I have nothing today. Asking God to provide what I need to not just survive, but thrive. This is the way of Jesus.

So round four begins today. Not ready physically but gaining strength spiritually, thank God. Praying that over you as well today.

Love and miss you all.

Paul

---

*God has a purpose for your pain,
a reason for your struggle, a reward for your
faithfulness. Don't give up.*
Dave Willis

Scripture reading.

I can do all this through him who gives me strength.

Philippians 4:13 (NIV)

Reflection.

We don't typically find out what God can really do in us until we run out of our own resources. When you've come to the end of yourself, that is where you usually find Jesus, and all of the resources of Heaven, waiting for you. He won't force himself on you. You need to ask God for this kind of strength.

Prayer.

God, I need you to be my source and supply of strength today. Give me what I need to not just survive, but even survive today. Amen.

22

Journal Entry for September 26, 2020.

Bitter or better?

Good morning, friends. Round four of chemo is officially behind us. I say "us" because I really consider that you are on this journey with me, and I am so grateful for that reality. Much love from Becky and me to you.

This next week is the tough week where blood counts go down, and the discomfort goes up. It's a process. I gotta be a good patient and do my part. Already starting to feel the effects of this previous round (*no bueno*) but believing all will pass quickly.

Reading through Philippians with a buddy and came across this passage in Philippians 4:4: "**Rejoice in the Lord always. I will say it again: Rejoice!**" Interesting verses to come across on this first day after chemo. Not the verse one would run to considering the circumstances but, alas, here it is.

Getting to the point quickly . . . I've lived life long enough to recognize God's Word comes to us at just the right time and place. Our job is to faithfully position ourselves to come to him daily. There is a cooperative dance between us and God most days. Sometimes, it's a fight. Sometimes, it's not a fight. Still, how many of us believe He's available as any loving Father should be? He's willing to sit with us, talk with us, encourage and breathe life into us in our time of need. *Are we willing to give him our "valuable" time?*

With all that is going on in my life (and I'm sure, in your life), do you see value in spending just a few minutes with God, allowing him to infuse the fruit of his Spirit into your life, *that is, love, joy, peace, patience, kindness, goodness, gentleness, faithfulness, and self-control?* **Do you believe that only God is the source and supply of the better and best life available to you AND through you each day?**

And so, I'm presented today with God's marching orders for the day, even within rather uncertain physical circumstances. I didn't choose this verse. It chose me today. I am called today to this spiritual challenge: "Rejoice in the Lord always. I will say it again: Rejoice!"

There is a choice that needs to be made. I can allow my circumstances to make me bitter or make me better. If left to my own strength, I am honestly convinced that I do *not* have enough in me to produce the "fruit" listed above. I've tried. I've failed. I know myself. I'm just not that good at it. Too much of me gets in the way. However, when I truly surrender to God daily and breathe out my last effort, emptying myself of my will, there is an opportunity to breathe in new and fresh life from God that fills my life with his resources, his gifts, his fruit, his energy, and his sustenance. When I take the time to practice this time with God in meditation, prayer, and contemplation, I find myself being rejuvenated and "Rejoiced." Joy is put back into me.

So there you go. That's how I started my day today. Praying for the same power and peace over you in whatever you're faced with.

Peace and love to you all.

Paul

You either get bitter or you get better. It's that simple. You either take what has been dealt to you and allow it to make you a better person, or you allow it to tear you down. The choices do not belong to fate, it belongs to you.
Josh Shipp

Scripture reading.

Rejoice in the Lord always. I will say it again: Rejoice! Let your gentleness be evident to all. The Lord is near.
Philippians 4:4-5 (The Message)

Reflection.

There is a choice that needs to be made. You can allow your circumstances to make you bitter or make you better. Choose today what your posture will be like. Ask God, who is near to you right now, to fill you up with all that you need today to be the better and best version of yourself, despite your physical circumstances.

Prayer.

God, fill me up with what is up there. I need it down here. I want to be the better and best version of myself today, regardless of my physical setbacks. Amen.

23

Journal Entry for September 28, 2020.

Help!

Update: These two days have not been so great. Guessing the toughest couple of days yet. Or maybe I'm just all up in my head right now . . . in a bad way.

Please pray for a better attitude for me. I need God's peace over my own.

I'm dizzy. Sore throat. Weak. Achy. Sleeping a lot. Ugh.

It's a process; I get it, but it just stinks. Not much of an update. I promised I'd be honest with you. ☹

Reflection.

Sometimes, you just need to vent. Sometimes, you just need to scream. Sometimes, you just need to "lament." A lament is a passionate expression of grief or sorrow. This is exactly what David often did in the Psalms, crying out to God because things were not okay in his life. That practice of lamenting eventually turns to praise. Seems ridiculous but that is the pattern we see. It's okay to not be okay today. It's okay to cry before God and tell him how lousy things are. He can handle it.

It's okay not to be okay. It's not okay to stay there.
Harry Hambley

Scripture reading.

O Lord, hear me as I pray; pay attention to my groaning. Listen to my cry for help, my King and my God, for I pray to no one but you. Listen to my voice in the morning, Lord. Each morning I bring my requests to you and wait expectantly.
Psalm 5:1-3

Prayer.

God, I hate what I'm going through right now. I cannot do this any longer. I don't have what I need to be what I need at this moment. I need help. Amen.

■□■

$$\left(24 \right)$$

Journal Entry for September 30, 2020.

Is it okay to be mad at God?

(Spoiler: I wrote this more for me than for you. Writing is good therapy for me. If you benefit from this, then praise God! Thanks for praying with us the past couple of days. It has been rough. Grateful to know you're standing with us.)

Is it okay to be mad at God? The short answer is "Yes." God can handle it.

The longer answer is still "Yes" but involves some deeper understanding of God's heart for intimacy with his children. We also have to understand that there are things that he sees that we just don't see *(sovereignty conversation)*. Our challenge—if we're honest—is really that we begin to lose confidence in God's ability to control circumstances, other people, and the way they, or life, affect us. We start to question why God would allow a good person to experience sickness and pain when we know that pain, sickness, and brokenness are the result of a fallen world, not because God has too much on His plate or is dropping the ball.

There is much to be said about sickness, pain, and brokenness but *the end game is always going to be the same—God at work in us and through us.* God's heart is intimacy with you and me. That was his heart back in Genesis. That is his heart through Scripture. That is his heart for you and me even as you read this. **As hard as it may be to hear or soak in, God will cause and/or allow anything to happen to us as a means to nudge us into his loving arms.**

Did I just say "cause?" I did. *Please don't hear what I am not saying.* I'm not saying God causes cancer. I don't believe he does. Cancer is yet another byproduct of a fallen and broken world that needs healing. Cancer sucks. I'm just saying that we have evidence in the Scriptures that God has caused *and* has allowed challenge in the lives of his people with a specific purpose: relational intimacy with his kids. That is all He wants—a deeply planted, uninterrupted, intimate, and loving relationship with you and me.

So yes, it's okay to be mad at God if you feel you need to be mad. He can handle it. We have a model for it in Scripture. Nearly a third of the Psalms are laments to God, deep expressions of anguish and grief. Writers who were frustrated, confused, perplexed, and disappointed at God all "said so" to God. I certainly have gone there even in these past couple of days. God's shoulders are broad and strong. He's not surprised, frustrated, or thrown off by your anger and frustration.

The challenge is this: **If you are mad at God, make sure you to talk *to* him rather than complaining *about* him**. Take a cue from the Psalms. Work your complaint through with God and give him a chance to show up and show off in your life.

I'll say it again, God is more interested in a relationship with you, even if it's a bit rocky from your perspective. C.S. Lewis writes that the reward of prayer (complaining to God is still prayer) is the presence of God. That is God's goal with you in the first place—his presence and ultimately his provision and power in and through your life. If things get ugly or challenging along the way, He's willing to go there with you, knowing the better and best version of you is on the other side of that tension.

Again, he can handle it. He can handle you. He loves you.

———————◼—◻—◼———————

. . . most people who are angry with God are angry with him for being God. They're not angry because he has failed to deliver what he promised; they're angry because he has failed to deliver what they have craved, expected, or demanded.
Paul David Tripp

Scripture reading.
And we know that God causes (or allows*) everything to work together for the good of those who love God and are called according to his purpose for them.
Romans 8:28 **My note added.*

Reflection.

Sometimes, God permits tragedy. Sometimes, he allows things to break apart and get messy. However, God will not allow tragedy to triumph over your life. He wants to triumph. He wants to give you what you need to win in a situation where you feel like you are at a loss. We must let God define what is good in our lives. We think the "good" is great health, no worries, and no pain. God believes that the "good" is, in this case, a relationship with Jesus, and a relationship with Jesus brings fruit that is good and healthy and right for our lives. He brings everything, even the bad stuff, together for *his* good, if we will allow him to. Take some time and pray this prayer below.

Prayer.

God, at this moment, in my disappointment, frustration, pain, and hurt . . .God, in all of this, I'm asking you to make sense of what doesn't make sense. I love you, God. I want what is best for me and my family. I'm asking you to cause everything that is messy to work together for my good, even if I don't immediately understand it all. I am willing to trust you right now for my tomorrow. Amen.

(25)

Journal Entry for October 5, 2020.

Strong week.

Update: I will keep this one brief. This week is again what we call the "strong week," meaning, all of my counts (white/blood cells primarily) are rebounding and stabilizing.

Should be getting a PET scan today letting us know a couple of things.

1. The tumor. We're hoping to see no tumor, the malignant subject of our story. :-(
2. Walls of the intestine. We're hoping to see a thick and healthy wall in my intestine.
3. Anything else. We're hoping we find nothing else.

If all of this above is good, then the rest of the treatment is about killing (chemo-ing) what we cannot see and making sure Mr. Pablo is good to do. If all is good above, then we're still on the road to having this thing behind us some time at the end of November, maybe the beginning of December.

Believing for *big* things this week. Friends, thank you for praying!

Paul

I am not in control. But I am deeply loved by the one who is.
Toby Mac

Scripture reading.

But God made the earth by his power; he founded the world by his wisdom and stretched out the heavens by his understanding.
Jeremiah 10:12 (NIV)

Reflection.

Do you believe that God created the heavens and the Earth by his own power? If so, then do you also believe that God can completely eradicate sickness from your body? Then pray for that? Keep in mind that his wisdom and understanding sometimes go a different way—still for our good. Still, we must pray for God's power to show up and show off in our lives. He wants an opportunity to demonstrate that power.

Prayer.

God, come and demonstrate your presence and power and provision in my life through physical healing and or spiritual healing. Amen.

26

Journal Entry for October 11, 2020.

I cannot do this any longer.

Good Sunday to you all. Wanted to give an update and then an encouragement.

Update.

Finally got the PET scan on Thursday. Insurance canceled it and then rescheduled it. Should know something tomorrow. Also starting round five of chemo tomorrow. A bit nervous as the last round was pretty rough. I'm feeling good today but naturally have a bit of anxiety starting another round tomorrow. Pray for strength and endurance on this one.

To that end, I've been thinking on Psalm 121 all this past week. I honestly don't want to do one more day of chemo. Been pretty transparent about that one. Who would want to? I get that my feelings are natural and to be expected. Still, Psalm 121 gets my head and I feel like God is trying to get a message to me. In the ancient Christian tradition, this particular Psalm was purposed to serve as a morning prayer. This Psalm can be used as an on-ramp for our day, regardless of what is in front of us.

Psalm 121: 1–2: "I lift up my eyes to the hills. From where does my help come? My help comes from the Lord, who made Heaven and earth."

The practice of meditating on God is a good practice. As I sit with God in the morning, redirecting my attention to a more divine source and supply of strength outside of myself, there is something in me (in us) that rises above current circumstances. This happens almost without fail. *As I lift my eyes to the hills above what is right in front of me, I recognize that there is something beyond me that wants to work within me to help me not just survive today but to thrive today.* God's power and presence is made possible to us and in us by way of Jesus's death and resurrection.

This is how it works in our lives:

We put behind (die to) our own strength, recognizing that what we have alone in us is not enough. At the same time, we pick up the strength of Jesus by way of the Holy Spirit stepping into and living out *his* grace-filled resources. So when we pick up God's strength, we are resurrected to a new way of thinking, acting, and living because the God of the universe is standing up inside of us, animating us to the better and best version of ourselves. *I can do NONE of this without Jesus who gives me strength (Philippians 4:13).* This is the way of Jesus.

So tomorrow morning, as I get up to do my day, as you get up to do your day, I'm praying that I will . . . that we will lift up our collective eye site to God and all of His resources. That we will look to *him* as the source and supplier of everything that we need and then some.

Remember, it's not just for our sake but for those that God is using us to impact. This is bigger than us.

Love and appreciate you all.

Paul

P.S. I'll let you know what we find out on the PET scan as soon as we know. PB

When you're going through hell, keep on going.
Never, never, never give up.
Winston Churchill

Scripture reading.
I look up to the mountains—
does my help come from there?
My help comes from the Lord,
who made heaven and earth!
He will not let you stumble;
the one who watches over you will not slumber.
Indeed, he who watches over Israel
never slumbers or sleeps.

The Lord himself watches over you!
The Lord stands beside you as your protective shade.
The sun will not harm you by day,
nor the moon at night.
The Lord keeps you from all harm
and watches over your life.
The Lord keeps watch over you as you come and go,
both now and forever.

Psalm 121

Reflection.

As I lift my eyes to the hills above what is right in front of me, I recognize there is something beyond me that wants to work within me to help me not just survive today but thrive today. Only God can make this a reality in my life and through my life.

Prayer.

God, we're praying that Heaven and Earth would collide in our lives. Give us a heavenly perspective for an earthly good this week. In Jesus's name, Amen.

27

Journal Entry for October 12, 2020.

Good news!

Hey, y'all, a quick update on PET scan. Short answer is that we went from a 32 to a 5 on the illumination scale. What does that mean? Means that the malignant tumor is barely seen now in the PET scan, which means it's super tiny and about gone. So far, we are not seeing anything else of concern.

We will do another PET after round six. Round five of chemo began today.

Everything else on the PET looks great. This is *very* good news. Thanks for praying. Keep it up!

Peace and love to you all.

Pastor Paul

Look for Christ and you find him.
And with him everything else.
C.S. Lewis

Scripture reading.
Let us hold fast the confession of our hope without wavering, for he who promised is faithful.
Hebrews 10:23 (ESV)

Reflection.
As a person of faith, it is important to be faithful to God, regardless of what we think the outcome will be. Faithfulness requires us to submit to the ways of God. His ultimate goal for us is friendship with him and his faithfulness orbits around that goal. Regardless of our physical condition, God's ultimate goal is our spiritual health. He cares about it all, but his heart is to capture our hearts for eternity. Where do you need God to increase your faith today?

Prayer.
God, increase my faith above all things and in all things. I want my friendship with you to increase. Help me depend on you and submit my ways to you. Amen.

28

The value of silence.

Good day to you friends. About done with yet another week of chemo, and so far, it has been very manageable—thank God. Trying to control side effects with diet and hydration and whatever exercise I can muster up. Seems to be working out. Of course, the drugs the docs pour on me are probably helping as well. Ha-ha!

I wanted to pass along what I received yesterday in a lovely card sent by a beautiful couple from our faith family (The Vineyard). I hope you are encouraged by this:

When we discover the secret of being inwardly at worship while outwardly at work, we find that the soul's silence brings us to God and God to us. Silence takes us beyond the limits of consciousness and into the heart and mind and will of God.

I've probably spent more time alone in the last three months than I have in the last twenty-seven years of family life. Remember that Becky and I have a bunch of kiddos so life among our family and friends doesn't always produce the "quiet life," as much as we love the life we have. It's been very quiet these past three months. Not that my family or friends haven't been there for me. They have and I've loved it. What a gift our kids, church family, and friends have been. THANK YOU!

For me, there have just been so many sleepless nights, early mornings, quiet walks, isolation, and quarantined times in the hospital while not feeling well . . . just me, myself, and I wrestling with and talking with God, contemplating so many abstract thoughts, ideas, Scripture, frustrations, fears, and a host of other emotions—good, bad, and ugly. It's been a journey to say the least.

More than anything, I'm learning to worship God all over again.

I'm learning to practice the presence of Jesus within every circumstance. It's been a challenging journey, but I'm relearning that the default hardwired in me *leans hard to* my desperate need for the fruit of God's Spirit (Galatians 5:22–23). By the way, *you* were wired this way too. We were not meant to live apart from God's presence and power in and working through our lives. This is what we were made for. John Piper says it beautifully: "God is most pleased with us when we are most satisfied with him." Do you know that I am *learning and leaning* in that direction all over again? That's got to be a good outcome of all of this, would you agree? I sure feel so.

You know that silence can be a gift if you sit with it well. As the quote continues above: "Silence takes us beyond the limits of consciousness and into the heart and mind and will of God." If I need to be alone, there is no other place I'd rather be than sitting in God's presence. It's in that place where we discover *the* peace that goes beyond all understanding. It's what you're longing for, reaching for, working for each day.

Praying that you find this peace wherever your life takes you today.

Love you all.

Paul

———————————————————————————■—□—■———————————————————————————

Sometimes, you gotta take a break from all of the
noise to appreciate the beauty of all of the silence.
Robert Tew

Scripture reading.

Always be full of joy in the Lord. I say it again—
rejoice! Let everyone see that you are considerate in
all you do. Remember, the Lord is coming soon. Don't
worry about anything; instead, pray about every-
thing. Tell God what you need, and thank him for
all he has done. Then you will experience God's peace,
which exceeds anything we can understand. His

peace will guard your hearts and minds as you live in Christ Jesus.

(Paul to the Church at Philippi, written while in jail, not fully knowing the future outcome.)

Philippians 4:4-7

Reflection.

You may be in a place of loneliness in this season. Sleepless nights. Early mornings. Restless moments where you feel you're desperate for a friend, but it may be some time before that friend or family member shows up. Can I challenge you to sit back, take a breath, and simply breathe in the presence of God with the prayer below?

Prayer.

God, I need your presence and power right now. Provide for me what I need at this moment. Give me the fruit of your Spirit and bring me closer to you right now. Amen.

$$\left(29\right)$$

Journal Entry for October 20, 2020.

The wounded healer.

Rough week this week so far. Asking God to minister to my heart using this quote today. So grateful that the Wounded Healer (Jesus) has gone before us in all suffering for us. Asking for *his* strength, *his* wisdom, *his* endurance, *his* courage. This is what Jesus does in us and through us when we abandon ourselves and our own strength, submitting to his power and presence at work.

"Nobody escapes being wounded. We are all wounded people, whether physically, emotionally, mentally, or spiritually. The main question is not, 'How can we hide our wounds?' So, we don't have to be embarrassed, but 'How can we put our woundedness in the service of others?' When our wounds cease to be a source of shame, and become a source of healing, we have become wounded healers." (The late Catholic priest and author Henri Nouwen)

Thanks for standing with us.
Peace and love to you all.
Paul

---

*The great illusion of leadership is to think that man
can be led out of the desert by someone who has
never been there.*
Henri Nouwen

Scripture reading.

In reference to our pain that Christ carried on the cross . . .

Just watch my servant blossom!
Exalted, tall, head and shoulders above the crowd!
But he didn't begin that way.
At first everyone was appalled.
He didn't even look human—
a ruined face, disfigured past recognition.
Nations all over the world will be in awe, taken aback,
kings shocked into silence when they see him.
For what was unheard of they'll see with their own eyes,
what was unthinkable they'll have right before them.
Isaiah 52:13-15 (The Message)

Reflection.

The beauty of the Gospel is that Christ took our suffering to the cross. The sickness, pain, disappointment, frustration, and hurt that results from a broken and fallen world were placed on Jesus in his suffering. He absorbed it. Does that mean we won't suffer or be sick, in pain, disappointed, frustrated, or hurt? No. But what it does mean is that these things don't have to have victory over our lives. They don't have to control us because they have been dealt with, once and for all, in the death and resurrection of Jesus Christ. He identifies with us in our suffering and, therefore, knows what we need in our suffering and can provide what we need.

Prayer.

Jesus, thank you for suffering on our behalf. You know what I need and can provide what I need in my suffering. So, Jesus, I give you my suffering and ask for your peace, patience, and perseverance in exchange. Amen.

(30)

Journal Entry for October 26, 2020.

Self-awareness.

Good Monday to you, friends. Well, this week has been "one for the books" as they say. I mentioned it was rough. It was. You should probably know that the effects of chemotherapy are cumulative, intensifying each round. That's what they told me and *oh my*, that is what I'm experiencing. So grateful to you all for uniting with us in prayer. Grateful indeed.

Thank God we only have one more round because this past week was *no bueno* at all. Still hurting a bit today but coming out of it to hopefully enjoy a good strong week this week, free to breathe before beginning chemo again Monday.

Big self-awareness moment this morning: I'm realizing something as I anticipate feeling better physically this week. My capacity for comfort tends to increase when my capacity for pain increases. *In other words, as pain and discomfort increase, so does my openness to receive relief from such pain and discomfort.* As I come to a place of wanting to give up, get out, or get through, and I recognize my powerlessness over my situation, I find myself (found myself) in a precarious posture of surrender . . . merely out of desperation over discipline. At moments, it was too much to bear. Seriously, nothing in the natural was helping. I found myself instinctively reaching for something beyond the natural.

Question: Is that what true worship should be like?

Was I worshipping last week? 'Cause, it didn't look like it looks at church with hands raised, voices singing, and church folk looking their Sunday best. Not even close. Was what I experienced worship? Is this what the apostle Paul meant when he encouraged us to rejoice always, pray without ceasing, and give thanks in *all* circumstances (1 Thessalonians 5:16–9)? He even throws an exclamation mark on it and says, ". . . for this is the will of God in Christ Jesus for you. Don't quench the Holy Spirit." Hard to argue when someone closes a sentence out that way.

Now, I guess I have to spend the rest of my life unpacking that reality in *all* circumstances. Thank God for *all* of God. I'm not strong enough to figure this one out on my own.

Worshipping with you this week.

Pastor Paul

What is necessary to change a person is to change his awareness of himself.
Abraham Maslow

Scripture reading.

Rejoice always, pray continually, give thanks in all circumstances; for this is God's will for you in Christ Jesus. Do not quench the Spirit.
1 Thessalonians 5:16-19 (NIV)

Reflection.

To be clear, God's will is not that you have sickness. Not at all. God's will is that we rejoice, pray continually, and give thanks in all circumstances. *This* is God's will for your life. Easier said than done but, nonetheless, still the direction of God. The obvious is this: you don't have what it takes to obey this directive. That's the point of the Gospel. You need help. I need help. We need help. That is where God's grace enters the scene and does its great work. Grace is God helping us where we need help simply because God loves us and wants to. True worship involves you giving God your mess and in exchange, he gives you his grace, love, compassion, comfort . . . and the list goes on.

Prayer.

God, my life is pretty messy right now. It sounds like you're willing to take my mess in exchange for your grace, love, compassion, and comfort right now. I'll take it. Thank you for doing for me what I cannot do in this season. Amen.

$$\left(\,31\,\right)$$

Journal Entry for November 2, 2020.

Just another purpose-filled experience?

Good morning, friends. I'm going in for round six of chemotherapy this morning. I have a lot of mixed emotions today. On the one hand, I'm so grateful this is the final round as they tell me. Hope that is, in fact, the case. We'll learn more in my final PET scan, scheduled for November 16th. On the other hand, I don't know that I physically have it in me to withstand the effects of another intense round. Each round is more intense than the previous. And friends, I would pay money, *big* money to let this week pass from me. Yet, on the other hand, this is a very brief moment in my/our history, and surely, I can handle a few weeks of discomfort, pain, and uneasiness when you consider a lifetime of otherwise of comfort and health. Mixed emotions.

Still, I'm here and here we go . . .

This week, I'm trying to focus on the overall narrative of what God is up to in and through my life, your life, our lives. It's important to see the big picture in order to circumnavigate the here and now. Would you agree? You see, you can't read the end of the story and really appreciate it without the impact of the plot. You also can't just read the beginning of the story because there's really no investment in the characters. Additionally, you cannot simply open the book and see what's going on in the middle of the story because then you're frustrated, and you don't know why certain things are happening. *You have to understand the entire narrative of the story to appreciate any given scene or chapter.*

What is God's over-arching narrative in my life?

It's the same as it is for anyone: To love him, enjoy him, and increase his reputation, making him known in this world. Or, to put it another way, to live as a cooperative friend of Jesus for the sake of someone else. *Anything that happens to me or through me should be viewed with that lens on.* Not saying this is easy by any stretch of the imagination but it *is* our reality as Christians. This is our calling. There is no other way to live if my hope is to live with purpose and to my highest and fullest potential.

So that is what I'm asking you to pray for this week. You can pray for ease of pain and discomfort, but those things will pass. I'll still take it. ;-) *What needs to gain momentum and strength, however, is God's reputation **within** my/our current circumstances.* That is really all that matters. So today is just another purpose-filled experience. It's not about me; it's about God and what *he* is up to in and through my life.

Love you guys.

Pastor Paul

———■—□—■———

Your greatest ministry will most likely come out of your greatest hurt.
Rick Warren

Scripture reading.

You are the light of the world. A town built on a hill cannot be hidden. Neither do people light a lamp and put it under a bowl. Instead, they put it on its stand, and it gives light to everyone in the house. In the same way, let your light shine before others, that they may see your good deeds and glorify your Father in heaven.

Matthew 5:14-16 (NIV)

Reflection.

Consider your life as a book and this season is a chapter or two or three. This is not the end of your story. If you're not dead, God is not done. If your purpose really is to love God and enjoy him forever, making his name known through whatever experience you're going through, what will that look like today? Easier said than done? Completely, the answer is "yes." What is being asked in your season of life could be one of the hardest things to accomplish. We need God to give us the strength to be sure. However, consider a simple smile and a thank you to a nurse. Offer an "I love you" to a family member. Being a "light" of God's love doesn't have to be expensive or elaborate but a simple gesture of goodness in a world that is ugly.

Prayer.

God, if I am a light to shine in this world, I need you to come and illuminate me. Give me strength. Continue to push hope into me, and give me the capacity to demonstrate your goodness to those around me. Amen.

Journal Entry for November 4, 2020.

I got nothing.

Sometimes, all I have the strength for is listening and not talking. So, God, I'm simply listening to you today.

"Those who live in the shelter of the Most-High will find rest in the shadow of the Almighty" (Psalms)

"So, let us come boldly to the throne of our gracious God. There we will receive his mercy, and we will find grace to help us when we need it most" (Hebrews)

Worry is worshipping your problems.
Prayer is surrendering your problem.
Aussie Dave

Scripture reading.

The Lord is my strength and my song;
he has given me victory.
Songs of joy and victory are sung in the camp of the godly.
The strong right arm of the Lord has done glorious things!
The strong right arm of the Lord is raised in triumph.
The strong right arm of the Lord has done glorious things!

Psalm 118:14-16

Reflection.

May your faith be renewed and your soul strengthened as you read these encouraging Bible verses filled with promise and hope!

Prayer.

God, I need your strong right arm to hold me up today. Amen.

$$33$$

God SUPER invades our NATURAL.

Good morning, my friends. Wanted to share with you a text I sent this morning to a good friend who has committed to pray for me. He has also extended that invitation to his friends to pray over me, somebody they really don't even know. They know my friend; they know his heart, so they know me and my faith and have committed to pray for me and my family. Here is the text I sent him, orbiting around how I'm feeling today, day four of chemotherapy. Sometimes, God doesn't make sense. But I'm grateful for the grace of the offers.

Good morning Friend. Thought I would give you an update on my health this week as I am absolutely blown away by the extra measure of grace given to me physically, day four. Out walking four and a half miles this morning. Thursday of chemo week is typically the day that I take a turn for the worse, but I feel fantastic so far. I'm sure that I will experience the side effects soon but for round six, I don't think I should be feeling this good but praising God that I am. I can only believe and understand that God's SUPER is invading my NATURAL and while I typically don't ever understand how God does it, I'm grateful that he does. I want to extend my thank you to you, your friendship, and your circle of friends for committing to pray for me. I'm absolutely humbled and in all at whatever God chooses to grace over me. Love you man. Have a great day!

And I love you all. Thank you for standing with us. The best is absolutely yet to come.

Paul

■ □ ■

The only way God can show He's in control is to put us into a situation that we can't control.

Steven Furtick

Scripture reading:

But I have spared you for a purpose—to show you my power and to spread my fame throughout the earth.

Exodus 9:16

Reflection.

This road you are on is not easy. You will have bad days. You will have good days. On those good days, try to enjoy them fully and consider them a gift. Savor those precious moments and relearn to appreciate how sweet life is. On those bad days, simply rest. It may be that on those rough days, all you can do is pray and depend on what only God can provide in his comfort, encouragement, and peace. But know this, God wants to bring his *super* into your *natural* on good days and bad days. He wants to show up and show off in and through your life. He can do it. He has done it. He wants to do it again for you.

Prayer.

God, give me the strength to open myself up to you. I know you want to show up and show off in and through my life. I want that. I need that. Use me on the good days and the bad days. Thank you for being with me at all times. Amen.

34

Journal Entry for November 11, 2020.

When God does something unexpected and personal!

Hello, friends. Checking in to say hi! We're happy to say that while we were expecting this week to be from hell, physically, it hasn't been as bad as we thought it would be. If you recall, the effects of chemotherapy are not only rough, they are cumulative in nature, becoming more intense than the previous round. We have been preparing ourselves for that imminent reality.

Praising God that this week has been manageable, to be sure. Still rough but the recovery seems to be happening faster than we anticipated. Thank you for praying on our behalf. We love you guys.

I'm reminded of the words of Australian activist Christine Caine when she speaks about God doing something unexpected *and* personal. She writes, "I love it when God does something so profoundly personal, that you know, that you know, that you know, he sees you. He does what only he can do to remind you that he is God and that there is no other. If you told anyone what he did, they probably wouldn't believe you. Makes me smile."

Becky and I have felt that this week. We believe God has met us in a very unexpected and personal way. We have simply felt God's presence and power in our lives and specifically in my physical body. We don't deserve anything more than anyone else and, in fact, to receive something less than what we expected was not in our expectation at all. We were prepared to experience what was expected. But nevertheless, God met us in a very personal and unexpected way this week. It's just not been as bad as we thought.

So this week God has done only what God can do. He meets us where we need to be met. We don't understand it. We cannot always articulate it in words. We just receive it and say "thank you" for what he does in and through our lives. Then, we pass it along where we can.

That is the way of faith, and we see this pattern throughout the ancient Scriptures.

Peace and love to you guys.

Paul

■ □ ■

Sometimes, the difficulties in our life are really opportunities; they are moments where God can break through and can show you that he is faithful.

He can show you his provision and his blessing is
coming to your rescue.
Sarah Lieberman

Scripture reading.

"Go out and stand before me on the mountain,"
the Lord told him. And as Elijah stood there, the Lord
passed by, and a mighty windstorm hit the moun-
tain. It was such a terrible blast that the rocks were
torn loose, but the Lord was not in the wind. After
the wind there was an earthquake, but the Lord was
not in the earthquake. And after the earthquake there
was a fire, but the Lord was not in the fire. And after
the fire there was the sound of a gentle whisper. When
Elijah heard it, he wrapped his face in his cloak and
went out and stood at the entrance of the cave.
1 Kings 19:11-16

Reflection.

There are times when God is going to do something unexpected in your life. In fact, this will most
certainly happen during this season of sickness in
your life. In the same way that you reach out to
our heavenly father on the more difficult days,
why not reach out as well on the more delightful
days? God is always present. He is ready to sit with
you in all seasons. That's what a good father does.
He cries with you when you need a shoulder. He
celebrates with you when all is good. Our God is

a relational God who simply wants to be with us. Embrace our good God in every season.

Prayer.

God, thank you for being a good God who sits with me in the bad times and celebrates with me in the good times. Thank you for not abandoning me in any season. Amen.

$$\left(35 \right)$$

Journal Entry for November 16, 2020.

This is not paradise!

Friends, I just came off of a *rough* weekend. I know my last post was a much more positive report, and I'm grateful for the window of "not-so-bad" that was beyond our expectations. It *did* get worse over the weekend. I'm feeling much better today and just returned from my PET scan that will hopefully tell us I'm free and clear of this nasty cancer. Will know those results on Thursday at the oncologist's appointment. Believing for the touchdown!

This weekend made me think of this truth: We are *not* living in paradise. *This* is not our paradise. I was reminded of this by Paul Tripp's devotion today. This is what he says: "If we don't keep the eyes of our hearts focused on the paradise that will come, we will try and turn this poor fallen world into the paradise it will never be. In the heart of every living person is the longing for paradise."

Here is the thing about paradise: the cry of a toddler who has just fallen down is a cry for paradise. The pain of aloneness is a cry for paradise. The pain associated with cancer's side effects is a cry for paradise. We long for the suffering, pain, loneliness, frustration, and fear to be gone and those longings are longings for paradise. Thanks to the power of God's presence (by way of his Spirit), we get to experience glimpses, shadows, moments, and even seasons of paradise, but paradise is not fully experienced here on earth. That day will come when Jesus comes and consumes all of history, putting all of the broken things back together again.

Until that day, we place our hope in the author of paradise, regardless of our good days or our bad days.

Thanks for standing with the Baldwins in the good/bad days this past season. Love you all.

───────────◼ ☐ ◼───────────

The fact that our heart yearns for something Earth can't supply is proof that heaven must be our home.
C.S. Lewis

Scripture reading.
Yet God has made everything beautiful for its own time. He has planted eternity in the human heart, but even so, people cannot see the whole scope of God's work from beginning to end.
Ecclesiastes 3:11

Reflection.

Think about all of those times where you hoped for something better, sweeter, more peaceful than what is. Perhaps it was a better future for yourselves, your kids, and your world. Perhaps it was health over sickness or peace over chaos in any given situation. What you were hoping for was a slice of paradise. This is the hope we have to look forward to in Heaven, but it's also a reality we get to experience in part here on earth in a relationship with Jesus.

Prayer.

God, thank you for making it possible to experience a part of Heaven in a relationship with you. Continue to fill me with hope and push out the hopelessness I sometimes experience. Amen.

36

Not there yet . . .

Hello. friends. Update on PET scan results:

As the title suggests, we're not there yet. Was hoping to be 100 percent free of this lymphoma, but, alas, we're not there yet. Received the results of my PET scan, and everything looks good, but one spot still "glows" on the radiology report. Not huge. In fact, it's very small but nevertheless there. Not entirely sure it's cancer. Could be. It's inconclusive at this point. Could be something related to the side effects of chemo. Could be, they say, that we took the PET scan picture too soon after a rough week of chemo and its effects. The plan then? We'll let the body bounce back a bit, get healthy, and then take another picture on December 15th just to be sure it's nothing . . . although it could be something . . . or not. :-) Yeah, my mind is doing summersaults about now. In summary, we need to wait a bit longer.

Disappointed? Yes. A bit emotional? Yes. Exhausted? Yes. Worried? Not going to lie . . . a lil bit. Losing hope? Absolutely not.

We're thinking of it this way: If we were setting out to have lost one hundred pounds by this week, we would have lost ninety-eight pounds by now. Did we meet our goal? Not completely. We actually accomplished quite a bit. We had good success. But we're not there yet. It just means we need to keep at it to lose the extra two pounds. That is where we are at.

We may get disappointed, emotional, exhausted (mentally), and even a bit worried, but we're going to lean on God. In fact, these emotions are our cue to intentionally lean one way over another. We lean into God when life leans into us. That is the gift we have in the way of faith. As people of faith, we have resources that the world does not have. *We have resources that turn worry into worship.*

Praying the disappointment, frustration, and worry in your life will trigger you to lean the same direction as us in this season.

Leaning together.

Paul

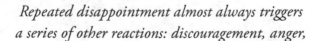

Repeated disappointment almost always triggers a series of other reactions: discouragement, anger,

frustration, bitterness, resentment, even depression.
Unless we learn to deal with disappointment, it will
rob us of joy and poison our souls.
Billy Graham

Scripture reading.

If you decide for God, living a life of God-wor-
ship, it follows that you don't fuss about what's on
the table at mealtimes or whether the clothes in your
closet are in fashion. There is far more to your life
than the food you put in your stomach, more to your
outer appearance than the clothes you hang on your
body. Look at the birds, free and unfettered, not tied
down to a job description, careless in the care of God.
And you count far more to him than birds.
Matthew 6:25-26 (The Message)

Reflection.

It's been said that worship is the antidote for
worry. And while the antonym of anxiety may
be assurance, the bridge across the great divide is
laced with worship. You cannot get from hopelessness to hope without worship. So what is worship?
It's putting God back in his rightful place as the
source and supplier of our peace, prosperity, provision, power, and, yes, assurance and hope.

Prayer.

God, I need you back in your place as the source and supplier of my hope. Too many things are crowding you out for your first place in my life. Please take over and take control of my peace. Be my provision and power to not just survive but thrive today. Amen.

37

Journal Entry for November 28, 2020.

Sore fingernails, a strange reminder.

Good morning, friends. An interesting couple of days, to be sure. Definitely getting stronger and healthier, feeling like the side effects of treatment are dissipating. That is good news. Feels good to feel good.

On the other hand, literally, are sore fingernails and toenails. A common issue and side effect of cancer and especially chemotherapy, sore fingernails and toenails can come about due to volatile cell activity coming and going as a part of the treatment process. Long story short, the nails are *super* weak and fragile and, of course, are sore. Weird.

And while the rest of my body is feeling like it's bouncing back and the pain and suffering associated with chemotherapy seem to be fading to a bad memory, the sore fingernails and toenails are still pretty present reminders that it wasn't/isn't a bad dream—reminders that it's very real, and it may not be over yet. Again, just keeping it real for ya'll.

There are days where I get in my bad headspace and wonder again, *What if this thing is not done? What if that small spot is* really *leftover cancer that needs to be dealt with?* Not a great place for my head to go when I think about hooking up with more chemo.

The reality is that we all have many reminders of our past hurts, suffering, pain, hang-ups, and even habits. Whether we brought that pain and suffering on ourselves or whether the pain and suffering were thrust upon us unjustly, the reminders are real and trigger bad headspace, responses, and even how we treat ourselves and others. I find that when I go to the bad headspace, I'm not always so compassionate with others. Why? To be honest, it's because I am preoccupied with my own issues—call it a selfish consumption. It's just hard to think about others when you're lost in your own very real, painful, unfortunate stuff. Not even a judgment. Just a reality of our humanity.

By the way, this is why the disciplines of devotion, meditation, and prayer are so important to our daily lives. At our church, we call it the first and ten. The first part of my day. The first ten minutes or more of my day. The first and ten are given to God each day so that *he* can fill my head with the stories that I need to tell myself so I can be the true me I was meant to be on any given day. It's a discipline that we practice to strengthen our spiritually dependent relationship with God. We need God to breathe certain truths into us daily:

That I am God's kid.

That *he* has a plan for me.

That his plan is good and grace-filled.

That I am fearfully and wonderfully made (Psalm 139:14).

That I am not dead, and *he* must not be done with me.

That there is purpose in the pain and that purpose is bigger than me.

Brené Brown calls it "The Story I Tell Myself." Every one of us tells ourselves stories. They are either true or false. I may still have cancer floating around in me. It could be a true story. But that reality does not own me, control me, or change God's plan in/through me. Also a true story if we believe the Scriptures. *I have to decide each day which stories are going to rule my world and perspective.* Do I want to live in a prison held captive by my own thoughts, or will I choose to live in a palace where God's rule and reign can captivate my thoughts to a new level?

It's true: my situation is not ideal. Neither is yours.

But our situation is not the truest thing about us. It does not define us but refines us. What is truer is that God is good and what he touches is good and what he is looking to accomplish is good and how he chooses to accomplish his plan is even better. While what is happening in my life, your life, may be true, it doesn't define you. God does. What he says about you is truer than whatever "truths" are floating around in your head.

So I have decided that every time I feel the pain of sore fingernails or toenails, I'm going to be reminded that I can go through this, or I can grow through this. I can get better over growing bitter. This is the way of Jesus following him both through suffering and through the resurrection. We *lean into* God when life leans hard into us.

Trusting whatever is sore in your life is serving as a trigger, stoking your imagination for what God is up to in and through your life.

Love you all.

Paul

Joy has nothing to do with the position of your body and everything to do with the posture of your heart.
Rachel Wojo

Scripture reading.

And I am convinced that nothing can ever separate us from God's love. Neither death nor life, neither angels nor demons, neither our fears for today nor our worries about tomorrow—not even the powers of hell can separate us from God's love No power in the sky above or in the earth below—indeed, nothing in all creation will ever be able to separate us from the love of God that is revealed in Christ Jesus our Lord.
Romans 8:38-39

Reflection.

What stories are you telling yourself in this season? Are they true stories? Are they made up? How do you know what's fiction or fact? I have found that reading Scripture is a good way to get the truest stories about who I am. Reading the pages of the Bible helps me understand who God really is and what God wants to do in and through me.

Prayer.

God, help me be convinced that nothing can separate me from your love. Not cancer, sickness, or anything else in this world. Overwhelm me with your presence and love today. Reveal yourself to me. Amen.

38

Journal Entry for December 3, 2020.

Asking for a tidal wave of prayer in an uncertain season.

Hey, ya'll. Thanks for standing with us in prayer and support. We love you all.

Update on the appointment today. Basically, there are two angles, and I'm not excited about either of the angles.

1. **COVID-19 is super crazy in Miami, so the oncologist has put the hammer down on me with respect to quarantine restrictions.** Wasn't doing much anyway but it's just getting old. No restaurants. No big crowds. Only close family. Still allowed to get back to work in the office on Tuesday, December 8 but not much more than that. Ugh! Anybody got a helicopter to get me to a private island??? :-)

2. **I had a rough, few days this past week, and, apparently, that is not normal at this point**. The chemo should be out of the body by now so any side effects should not be there either. Perhaps a couple of "aftershocks" but nothing like what I experienced on Monday where I was *big-time* nauseated with some pretty intense aching in the gut area. *No bueno*. That's a concern for the doctor, so they're trying to accelerate some testing, scanning, and so on this next week.

    Again, nothing really new but the intensity of the doctor's demeanor was concerning nevertheless. She's just doing her job to protect me and stay on top of protecting me. I appreciate that, and I guess it kind of annoys me at the same time. The appointment just launched me in*to the story I'm telling myself* headspace, which isn't always pretty for me. Recall the last letter on the topic of *the story I'm telling myself.*

- I know there is the possibility that the cancer is not fully gone yet. I get it.
- I know what chemo feels like and am UNINTERESTED in doing it again.
- I know the COVID-19 pandemic is a BIG concern for our culture.
- I know I need to be careful, cautious, and calculated.
- I'm ready to dive back into society, ministry, family life, and so on. Not allowed to do it. I get it.

- I'm tired of the ever-present worry that my family carries.

It's just getting old and the *waiting* period is driving me crazy. *Asking for a tidal wave of prayer over the next couple of weeks.* **Please spread the word. I/we need the prayer covering. The uncertainty is heavy on my heart.**

Sorrow looks back, worry looks around,
and faith looks up.
Ralph Waldo Emerson

Scripture reading.
(This may be a bit much, but I desperately need this today . . . and maybe you do too.)

Here are ten Bible verses to encourage you during uncertain times:
I'm not saying I'm super excited about them all, all of the time. Just saying that while I'm fighting it a bit, I am *leaning* into them nevertheless. I've lived long enough to know that this is the way to the best of my life for the rest of my life.

1. "God is our refuge and strength, always ready to help in times of trouble. So we will not fear when earthquakes come and the mountains crumble into the sea" (Psalm 46:1).

2. "Don't worry about anything; instead, pray about everything. Tell God what you need, and thank him for all he has done. Then you will experience God's peace, which exceeds anything we can understand. His peace will guard your hearts and minds as you live in Christ Jesus" (Philippians 4:6–7).

3. "Give all your worries and cares to God, for he cares about you" (1 Peter 5:7).

4. "The Lord will keep you from all evil; he will keep your life. The Lord will keep your going out and your coming in from this time forth and forevermore" (Psalm 121:7–8).

5. "So don't worry about these things, saying, 'What will we eat? What will we drink? What will we wear?' These things dominate the thoughts of unbelievers, but your heavenly Father already knows all your needs. Seek the Kingdom of God above all else, and live righteously, and he will give you everything you need. So don't worry about tomorrow, for tomorrow will bring its own worries. Today's trouble is enough for today" (Matthew 6:31:34).

6. "The Lord gives his people strength. The Lord blesses them with peace" (Psalm 29:11).

7. "Don't be afraid, for I am with you. Don't be discouraged, for I am your God. I will strengthen you and help you. I will hold you

up with my victorious right hand" (Isaiah 41:10).

8. "So be strong and courageous! Do not be afraid and do not panic before them. For the Lord your God will personally go ahead of you. He will neither fail you nor abandon you" (Deuteronomy 31:6).

9. "Give your burdens to the Lord, and he will take care of you. He will not permit the godly to slip and fall" (Psalm 55:22).

10. "Dear brothers and sisters, when troubles come your way, consider it an opportunity for great joy. For you know that when your faith is tested, your endurance has a chance to grow. So let it grow, for when your endurance is fully developed, you will be perfect and complete, needing nothing" (James 1:2–4).

Peace and love to you guys.

Paul

Reflection.

The Bible is filled with over 3,000 promises to you and me. Take some time to read through each verse again and write one simple promise for each verse.

Prayer.

God, give me the strength to believe what I'm reading about you. Fill me with your hope that the best is yet to come! Amen.

$$\textbf{39}$$

Journal Entry for December 8, 2020.

Challenging *and* good news? We'll see . . .

Hey, gang, quick report. I had some complications yesterday (Monday) that led me to the ER last night. Some pain in the abdomen that was not normal, which led to me spending the night, and it's looking like I will be here probably through Thursday.

The challenging news is that I'm back in the hospital. Don't love that.

The good news is that all of the tests are being moved up since I'm here. PET scan, endoscopy, and a few other tests that I cannot spell or pronounce—all moved up. This is good as it will give us solid answers and a clear picture of where we are at. We'll have those answers *this* week. That's good.

Asking for prayer that all comes back clean and clear. If not clean and clear, asking for a solid and manageable pathway toward the tail end of this journey.

Thanks for your faithfulness to me and my family. Love you all.

Paul

Anywhere peace is lacking, you can be sure the enemy is at work.
Priscilla Shirer

Scripture reading.

When I am afraid, I put my trust in you.
Psalm 56:3 (NIV)

Reflection.

Uncertainty is a difficult place to be. Most of us would rather know what the outcome is—even if bad news—than to not know. Uncertainty leads to fear, which is often rooted in a lack of control. We cannot control the outcome so we fear the worst. As you read the Bible, you will see that fear is often treated with love. It's the love of God that pushes out fear. Will I trust that God loves me enough to handle whatever needs to be handled in the best way that it can be handled?

Prayer.

God, help me in this uncertain time. If I am honest, I am afraid. Overwhelm me with your love and reassure me of your care for me. I cannot do this without you. Amen.

(40)

Journal Entry for December 10, 2020.

Progress but still uncertain.

Okay, here is the brief summary after two days of testing, talking, and collaboration between departments/doctors.

Everything is looking good. There is still "evidence" of lymphoma in that small awkward area of the small intestine (the mid area just under ribs). When we began, the rating on the radiology report was 32. It's now at 4.5. After meeting with the oncologist, the gastroenterologist, and internal medicine, they all agree that anything under a rating of 5 brings a lower suspicion of lymphoma. That's a very positive thing. It doesn't mean it's not lymphoma. It could be what is called *necrosis*, which is a decaying of the skin from treatment, or dead tissue. *WE'RE HOPING/ PRAYING FOR THIS*. If this is the case, I'm officially in remission, and the treatment is done; and we'll continue dealing with some soreness and inflammation in the intestine at the GI level.

What's next? Well the GI is going to do an endoscopy tomorrow to get one more picture, and they'll also take a biopsy to decide if it is or it isn't lymphoma.

If it is lymphoma, then we'll continue with chemo to get that last bit of cancer out. We'll provide more details on that if this is the case. For now, I'm here in the hospital through Tuesday morning just to be safe and sure.

Please pray that this is dead tissue and not any more lymphoma. Got *loads* of people praying. We are so encouraged by that!

Paul

In a culture like this, we're not going to accidentally slip into a healthy mindset; instead, we're going to have to actively work for it.
Jen Hatmaker

Scripture reading.

Therefore, since we have been justified through faith, we have peace with God through our Lord Jesus Christ, through whom we have gained access by faith into this grace in which we now stand. And we boast in the hope of the glory of God. Not only so, but we also glory in our sufferings, because we know that suffering produces perseverance; perseverance, char-

acter; and character, hope. And hope does not put us to shame, because God's love has been poured out into our hearts through the Holy Spirit, who has been given to us.

Romans 5:1-5 (NIV)

Reflection.

One promise that is consistent in Scripture is that in a relationship with Jesus, you have resources like hope. Hope is a powerful thing in suffering because it produces perseverance, which helps us become the people that we were meant to be, developing a character that is strong, hope-filled, and full of life. Isn't that what you want for yourself, for your family? This is what hope does.

Prayer.

God, fill me with your hope and help me become the person you designed me to be. Even when things don't work on my timeline, give me a posture that perseveres. Amen.

(41)

Trusting God when the lights are still turned off.

Today we will hopefully learn the results of yesterday's biopsy procedure and whether the subject tissue is *malignant* or *benign*. I say "hopefully" because nothing is ever on time when you're dealing with so many doctors, tests, procedures, and so on. Not blaming anyone. It's just complicated, and I get it. I run a large organization, and it's just a reality that the larger the issue, the more complicated, messy, and twisted things can become.

Today will be a *big* day of discovery, regardless of the actual outcome. If it's malignant, we keep going with chemo. If it's benign, we do the happy dance and begin the road to recovery. Keep praying, ya'll. So grateful that you all are standing with Becky, the kids, and myself in this season. Still floored with humility in it all.

So we're waiting and, in a sense and on some levels, we feel as if the lights are still turned off. In other words, we cannot see what God always sees. I don't know what the doctors are thinking unless, of course, they tell me. Heck, half the time, I'm not even sure what I really think about all of this. Many days it's an emotional roller coaster because I cannot see what I cannot see and wish I could just get a glimmer of light to see what's next. *Wondering if you can relate to this in your life at some level?*

But alas, we sit in the dark. It's a disruption, to say the least. Or is it?

This thought occurred to me this morning: **Is it possible that this disruption is actually a divine appointment?**

I dialed up this reality again remembering a great point from this past weekend at the Vineyard. The sermon point ran like this: "**Our DIS-appointment is HIS-appointment**" (emphasis mine). In the economy of God, what we often perceive as a dis- or missed appointment is often God's divine appointment. Read just a few passages of Scripture, and you'll see this pattern in real-time.

Of all of the Scripture available to us, Psalm 13 is probably the perfect pattern we should follow in our faith walk. Whenever the tension pokes us with impatience, Psalm 13 reminds us that the DIS-appointment is our cue that HIS-appointment is engaging, and God is about to show up and show off in a big way. While the lights may be off, God has night goggles and is active and at work doing what he does best. Psalm 13 reminds us that if we can *get* that God has a bigger perspective in mind, that God's greatest story is in play, it may just help us and lead us through the tension of the disruption to get a glimpse of God at work in us, around us, and even through us and beyond us.

May we be trained to trust God when the lights are seemingly still off, to know that God's light is always on, that he knows where he's taking us, and the best is yet to come, regardless of the outcome.

Love you all.

Paul

Believers talk about trusting in the Lord with their whole hearts and refusing to lean on their own understanding, but no one really knows what that means until circumstances cast them headfirst into a dark and painful place. If we give ourselves fully to God in those moments, we will obtain keepsakes of him to treasure now and forever.

Dr. David Jeremiah

Scripture reading.

Psalm 13: For the director of music. A psalm of David.

How long, Lord? Will you forget me forever?
How long will you hide your face from me?
How long must I wrestle with my thoughts

and day after day have sorrow in my heart?
How long will my enemy triumph over me?

Look on me and answer, Lord my God.
Give light to my eyes, or I will sleep in death,
and my enemy will say, "I have overcome him,"
and my foes will rejoice when I fall.

But I trust in your unfailing love;
my heart rejoices in your salvation.
I will sing the Lord's praise,
for he has been good to me.

(NIV)

Reflection.

Whenever the tension of life pokes us with impatience, Psalm 13 reminds us that the DIS-appointment is our cue that HIS-appointment is engaging, and God is about to show up and show off in a big way. While the lights may be off, God has night goggles and is active and at work doing what he does best.

Prayer.

God, give me eyes of faith over eyes of fear. Help me see your divine appointment in my disappointment. Amen.

42

Journal Entry for December 17, 2020.

Coming up for air.

Friends. Going to give you the short version and will expand later.

Today's appointment confirmed Tuesday's biopsy report findings that there are no traces of lymphoma in my body, and, therefore, no more need for chemo. Praising God BIG TIME!

Over the next three months, I get to breathe easy and get strong again. Stoked about that! I say three months because they *do* want to do the PET scan again soon. The intensity and sensitivity of my particular case warrant it. The doctors want to be sure. So they are not officially saying I'm in remission just yet, but it's looking very good. 😎 😃 👍 😌

For now, it's going to be a Merry Christmas in the Baldwin home.

Stay tuned as this thing unfolds a bit more.

Peace and love to you.

Paul

The deepest level of worship is praising God in spite of pain, thanking God during a trial, trusting Him when tempted, surrendering while suffering, and loving Him when He seems distant.
Rick Warren

Scripture reading.

Let everything that has breath praise the Lord. Praise the Lord.
Psalm 150:6 (NIV)

Reflection.

If you've been around church or faith for any length of time, you're most likely familiar with this verse. Never has this verse meant more to me than after having encountered the reality of death. May there never be a day that goes by that is absent of praise for a God who gives life.

Prayer.

God, THANK YOU for giving me breath to breathe and life to live. I never want to take it for granted. Help me live each day in the fullness of your love! Amen.

(43)

Journal Entry for December 21, 2020.

Mixed emotions.

Friends, I promised I would get you a more detailed update.

Thursday, we learned that the results of the biopsy report were, in fact, negative, meaning the doctors were not able to find any traces of lymphoma in my body. That's good news! It's been a *long* five months but grateful the process worked! *So, for now, it would appear that I am cancer-free and chemo-free.*

I say "for now" because the way the report technically reads, there is still cautionary fine print that warrants a watchful eye for the next three months; the oncologist is not ready to say that I'm in remission. In three months, I will have another PET scan to make sure I'm clean and clear of this thing. I also need to remain in quarantine because of the intensity of the COVID season. Because of the type of chemo I had, I'm severely immunodeficient for up to a year, and while we're doing things to improve that reality, I need to stay away from people until we can improve my immune system. I'm on the priority list for the vaccine so things may change if/when that happens. For now, I'm free from lymphoma and chemo but not free to move on with life. Kind of a weird paradox.

I can live with this but also find myself these past few days living in the tension between elation and frustration. I'm elated, relieved, and grateful that the process has worked. This past season has probably been the most difficult of my life. It's a bit surreal and, in some ways, hard to believe. I'm also frustrated because I want to get moving on life, work, and ministry but need to wait.

Don't hear what I'm not saying.

The good outweighs the bad here without question. Just remembering this morning that in a world that often seems out of control, it's comforting to know that God has things under control and he is my source of comfort, compassion, and encouragement.

No matter how many victories we receive in life, there will always be disappointments in one form or another. It's just the reality.

Today, I'm exploring my freedom. At one level, I will certainly live in the physical freedom. At another level, I will continue to *lean* into the spiritual freedom that brings love, joy, peace, patience, kindness, goodness, and faithfulness. This is what God does as we invite his presence and power to show up and show off in and through our lives.

Peace and love to you all.

Paul

God will test you because He wants you to mature. He wants you to develop a walk with him that is not based on your fluctuating emotions but on your commitment to Him as you learn to walk by faith.
Greg Laurie

Scripture reading.

But the fruit of the Spirit is love, joy, peace, forbearance, kindness, goodness, faithfulness, gentleness and self-control. Against such things there is no law. Those who belong to Christ Jesus have crucified the flesh with its passions and desires. Since we live by the Spirit, let us keep in step with the Spirit. Let us not become conceited, provoking and envying each other.
Galatians 5:22-26

Reflection.

It is worth repeating. Today, I'm exploring my freedom. At one level, I will certainly live in the physical freedom. At another level, I will continue to *lean* into spiritual freedom that brings love, joy, peace, patience, kindness, goodness, and faithfulness. This is what God does as I invite his presence and power to show up and show off in and through my life.

Prayer.

God, I know that someday I will be with you face to face in Heaven. I'm grateful for that. I'm also hope-filled that you bring Heaven to Earth through the work of your Spirit. Help me to open myself up to receive that from you today. Amen.

44

Do I have amnesia?

Good morning, friends. I thought I would offer an update on the heels of a not-so-great weekend mentally.

It's funny how we are in our humanity. There are seasons where God clearly gives us victories. We celebrate. We do the happy dance. This may last for a day or two. Then, we get frustrated, discouraged, or dismayed by the smallest thing. I'm talking about inconsequential things. You misplace your keys. A small project you are working on doesn't go your way. Someone in your family says something that is misinterpreted and gets you sideways.

Small things that trigger us in a big way. This was my weekend following one of the most hallowed of holidays of all days—Christmas. Crazy.

I mean, I literally just came off of a tidal-wave-journey of pain, suffering, uncertainty, and confusion—all while experiencing God's matchless and consistent grace throughout it all. Right? For now, the cancer is seemingly absent from my body. Praise God! *Rarely was there a day where I didn't see God at work, shining his light even when it was clearly dark all around.* And this past weekend was as if I had forgotten it all. Not completely. This is how we are in our humanity. We quickly, albeit momentarily, come down with amnesia, for lack of a better analogy.

In a nutshell, this is why I need the Scriptures *daily*. The ancient Scriptures remind me of the grander, more magnificent, story at work in and through me each day, despite me. The Scriptures remind me that God's story, his story, is my story, and the greater theme of redemption and reconciliation pursues me even when I am temporarily absent-minded. His story is our story. Even when we are unfaithful, God is still faithful . . . in the *big* victories (beating cancer) and in the small victories (peace in the midst of losing my keys).

To sum it up, I overheard some music Becky was listening to yesterday. The artist was Lauren Daigle. They were the words to the song, "Remember," and they were a testament to God's faithfulness, consistency, and goodness, even when we can't see it.

May this be our prayer and posture this next season, no matter what.

Peace and love to you all.

Paul

In the movie of life, nothing matters except our King and God. Don't let yourself forget. Soak it in and keep remembering that it is true. He is everything.
Francis Chan

Scripture reading.

But thanks be to God, who always leads us as captives in Christ's triumphal procession and uses us to spread the aroma of the knowledge of him every-where.

2 Corinthians 2:14

Reflection.

In our humanity, we live in a constant tension of the natural and the supernatural. In our flesh, we want what we want, and we see what we want to see. As we cooperate with God's Spirit, we want what he wants and we see what he sees. Like a preview of a blockbuster movie, we experience a taste of what is to come in the fruit of the Spirit. However, we have not fully experienced all of God's goodness just yet. Until then, we stay as close to God experiencing all that he is willing to give us.

Prayer.

God, continue to pursue me and fill me and walk with me. I want to live in the fullness of your grace in all that I do. Amen.

$$\left(45\right)$$

Am I winning or whining?

Hey, friends. I thought it would be a good time to offer an update on my physical and spiritual health.

Physically, this has been the first week where I have felt great. While I am (we are) free from lymphoma, the subject area (remember the jejunum, that small area of the intestine right after the stomach?) has really been pounded on because of the chemo. Not so fun.

I am certainly glad there is no cancer for now, but, oh my, that little space has created some issues. However, it's looking like it's doing much better, even though it certainly needs some more time to heal up. I have completely changed my diet to a plant-based diet, which definitely seems to be helping. Eating more meals per day and less in each meal. This is probably a better way to go anyway but certainly an adjustment. Feeling *very* good though.

I'm even growing facial hair after six months. I feel like I'm going through puberty all over again. Kidding . . . not really kidding. ;-)

Spiritually, it's been an interesting ride these past couple of weeks. This question has been floating in my head, and I'm not sure what to do with it: "Am I winning or am I whining?"

Again, with all of the victory God is giving us in this past season—both in physical healing and in family, church, business, and so on—anyone looking in from the outside would say, "Boy, get your head out of your booty and see that God is at work doing a great thing in your life!"

But I'm a human and humans tend to get wrapped up in their own stories outside of the ever-present help of God's grace. I gotta remember that I can do nothing apart from Jesus (John 15:4–5) but create a mess in my head and in life (I added that last part). You know it's true!

So I'm asking you to continue to pray for the Baldwin family. I'm good. We're good. I just want to continue to get better, and when I say "better," I mean that I want the better and best version of myself and ourselves for the sake of God advancing his Kingdom agenda. Yes, I'm asking for physical healing but probably more than that, I'm asking for spiritual healing. I'm trying to remember, if I'm still around, God's not done with me. That one idea has lifted my spirit more times than I can count these past few months. I don't exist for myself. I exist as a conduit of God's amazing and matchless grace for the benefit of someone else. I don't want to get in the way of that. Will you pray for that reality to increase in us?

Grateful to all of you for your prayerful support and love and encouragement.

Paul

Don't whine, whistle.
Marty Rubin

I used to think I could shape the circumstances around me, but now I know Jesus uses the circumstances to shape me.
Bob Goff

Scripture reading.

Remain in me, and I will remain in you. For a branch cannot produce fruit if it is severed from the vine, and you cannot be fruitful unless you remain in me. Yes, I am the vine; you are the branches. Those who remain in me, and I in them, will produce much fruit. For apart from me you can do nothing.
John 15:4-5

Reflection.

The reality is that God can change this world without us. He doesn't need our help. However, he chooses to work through humanity. He chooses to cooperate with people to reach people with his matchless love and grace. Our job is to become cooperative friends of Jesus for the sake of someone else. To do that, we need God's help. That is what grace does in our lives. Grace helps us become the better and best version of ourselves for the sake of those around us.

Prayer.

God, create a restlessness in me that will not go away until I re-align myself to you. I want to remain in you, receive from you, be filled by you, and be used by you so that others will fall in love with you. Amen.

46

Journal Entry for January 16, 2020.

I will give thanks to God when I don't have enough.

Good day to you all. Thought I would share this video that was shared with our staff. It ministered to my heart today. Search YouTube for "Housefires – I'll Give Thanks, featuring Kirby Kaple (Official Music Video).

───────────■ □ ■───────────

God is going to work it all out for the good. All the pain, frustration, heartbreak. Somehow and in some way, He is going to use all of the broken pieces to make a beautiful masterpiece.
Ashley Hetherington

Scripture reading.

And God is able to bless you abundantly, so that in all things at all times, having all that you need, you will abound in every good work.

2 Corinthians 9:8 (NIV)

Reflection.

God doesn't worry, so why do we worry? Such a good question if we really believe that God has got this, whatever you're going through. Commit today to choose to be thankful, knowing that he's got you covered. Choose thankfulness over worry today.

Prayer.

God, at this moment, I'm asking you to fill me with a heart of thankfulness over worry. Remind me of who you are and what you're doing in my life through it all. Overwhelm me with your goodness today. Amen.

Your faith is like . . .

This text came from a friend of mine yesterday (Romi Diaz). I was so stoked to have received it as he said everything I needed to hear at that moment. So grateful for a divine community surrounding us, willing to stand with us, loving us through prayer, and providing an encouraging word. Here is what my friend offered me today.

> *I truly hope you can find the time and the way to spend a few days with your surfboard and Bible. The act of surfing can animate so many spiritual truths and teachings it will blow your mind.*
>
> *Your faith is like your board, and you must stand on it and direct it in order for it to work at its highest potential.*

After a massive wipeout and a two to three-wave hold down (like my cancer battle), you come up barely breathing and exhausted physically, emotionally, and or spiritually. Get out of the danger zone (go into remission). Then, just breathe and assess your situation. Don't worry about ministering to others; you have no breath or strength right now. If you don't just breathe, you can drown . . . so comply.

Sometimes, your leash snaps, and your board floats away (as in the lifeline to your faith broke). Assess if it's safer to go after your board (save the vehicle of your faith) or make it to shore (a spiritual and physical safe space) without it and then get the help of lifeguards (pastors) and/or other surfers (your faith family).

Your board (faith) may have completely broken (or is in need of repairs or to be replaced). You might need help getting in. Call the lifeguards (pastors and mentors) or other surfers (brothers and sisters in Christ).

And sometimes, the whitewater (remnants of the thing that tried to take you out) will lead you to shore . . .

Once on shore, you might throw up and or pass out from exhaustion (let it all out, purge yourself from the emotions, and lie still as you regroup).

Hydrate (replenish your mind and spirit).

Rest (be restored physically, spiritually, and emotionally).

Repair or replace your equipment, your leash (lifeline) and board (vehicle of faith).

Match your skill (knowledge, faith, and capacity) to your equipment and your wave choices. If Waimea (cancer) almost took you out, do not paddle out there again (listen to your doctor about prevention and staying healthy).

If you have outgrown a shortboard (increased your faith), then increase the size of your board (vehicle of faith).

If you're out of shape, train (build stamina physically, emotionally, and spiritually) before paddling out into the big surf again (life's full-on challenge)!

Love you, bro!

Wasn't that beautiful? My prayer for you today is that you receive what you just read for your own life. I pass on what has been given to me in hopes that God will arrest your spirit today.

Peace and love to you all.

Pastor Paul

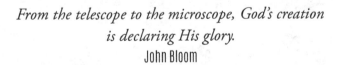

From the telescope to the microscope, God's creation is declaring His glory.
John Bloom

Scripture reading.

Taste and see that the Lord is good; blessed is the one who takes refuge in him.
Psalm 34:8 (NIV)

Reflection.

The reality of God is that he is in all of creation. You don't have to look too far to see a creator at work. Look out the window and see the mountains, the ocean, a river, or the vast plains of the Midwest. It doesn't matter where you live, there is beauty all around you. In fact, you can look in the mirror and see the miracle of our Maker if you see what he sees.

Prayer.

God, help me see what you see in this world around me. Remind me how close to me you are in creation. Remind me that you have everything under your command and control. Amen.

(48)

Journal Entry for January 30, 2020.

It's a process.

Good morning, friends. Thought I would update you all on my progress. It's been a few days since I've last written.

Still waiting for the March 2nd PET scan. This is the scan that will either give us permission to say I'm officially in remission or give us direction for more treatment. Yes, I'm nervous. Yes, I'm content. :-) Will keep you posted.

In the meantime, the subject area (remember that part of the intestine that caused all of this trouble?) seems to be calming down. If you will recall, the chemo did some damage to this area that was littered with lymphoma. It was an aggressive attack that called for aggressive treatment. I recently learned that because I was so healthy and handling the treatment so well, they decided to push the gas pedal on treatment and give me as much as I could possibly withstand. Fun!

Well, it seems to have done its work, which is the good news. The more challenging news is that it beat the marbles out of that particular area, and they are not sure if it's just scar tissue or swelling or something else. Again, the March 2nd PET will give them an idea of what is going on. Still, these past two weeks I have felt strong, healthy, and back to normal. Still growing hair again at a rapid rate. So all seems like it's moving in the right direction.

I'm still in quarantine as the oncologist remains super cautious during this COVID season. Grateful to God and to the Vineyard that we were able to set up my ability to manage things entirely from home, meeting with my staff virtually, and taking good advantage of every bit of technology (thank you PJ Ashenfelter at Notre Dame) available to us.

Want to continue to express my/our gratitude to you all for your faithfulness in prayer, your encouraging words, cards, and the texts. You all continue to humble this Baldwin family.

Peace and love to you.

Paul

Faith is not believing in my own unshakable belief,
faith is believing in an unshakable God.
Beth Moore

What we are waiting for is not as important

as what happens to us while we are waiting.
Trust the process.
Mandy Hale

Scripture reading.

But those who trust in the Lord will find new strength. They will soar high on wings like eagles. They will run and not grow weary. They will walk and not faint.

Isaiah 40:31

Reflection.

Physical and spiritual growth is a process. How can you trust a process? If you were physically training, would you trust your trainer? Depends on her faithfulness. Did she let you down? Has she proven her worth as your trainer? Same idea with God. We trust God because he has been faithful, never letting us down. We'll trust him again and again, regardless of our physical and emotional situation. We know that we know that we know God will show up and show off in our lives.

Prayer.

God, please give me the tenacity to trust you. Give me strength. Help me to not grow weary or faint as the Scriptures tell us. I need more of you in my life. Amen.

(49)

Journal Entry for February 7, 2021

A final and more elongated summary/thought . . . for now.

How can I make sense of my darkest valleys?

This journey has been a battle. It's been a physical battle, obviously. My body has gone through more than I ever thought it could handle. It's been agonizing, painful, even unbearable on many days. There were days where I would have preferred, albeit probably irrationally, to see it all end. Yes, physically, this has been a battle.

It's been a battle emotionally too. This journey has been lonely, frustrating, and confusing for me and my wife and kids. Remember that much of this journey happened in the hospital under quarantine during the COVID-19 season. I was not able to physically be with Becky or the kids.

The battle physically and emotionally certainly led to a brutal battle spiritually. While I warred for my commitment to remain devout in my doubt, please hear me when I say that I absolutely had doubt. This is the entire point of this letter (now a devotional). I've asked God more logical and illogical questions than I've ever asked anyone, ever!

To put it another way, this season has been one of the darkest valleys I've ever walked through, but the difference-making element in this journey has been the light that has gone with me: my wife and my kids. And while the light of hope may have flickered and been perceivably dim at times, it never went out. I have grown to cherish the words of Pastor Rick Warren of Saddleback Church and his description of God at work in the valleys: "God is God, not just of your mountaintop experiences, he's the God of the valleys too!" Perfectly stated.

Friends, God looks into every dark valley you could possibly encounter, and he asserts this reality: *I am the God of the valleys. I'm not just a God of the good times in your life. I'm not just a God of the happy times in your life. I'm not just a God when everything's going smoothly. I'm the God of the valleys too!*

So I want to land the plane on this devotional about valleys, even your darkest valleys. Why?

Because valleys are a part of life.

They are just realities that everyone encounters. You cannot escape them. In my early young adult years, I used to work on a tugboat crew, and getting seasick was a reality of working on the ocean. You could say that getting seasick was an occupational hazard. If you spend any amount of time on the ocean, it's just a reality. My captain, a forty-four-year-sea-faring veteran, put it this way: "People who say they never get seasick are either liars, or they just haven't gotten sick yet. It will happen. I promise."

He always had a smile of certainty when he made comments like that. Getting seasick when you work on the ocean is just part of it. In the same way, if you've spent any amount of time on planet Earth, you've certainly experienced some kind of a valley. If not, you will. I'm sorry to sound depressing, but valleys simply happen to everyone. Many of you would describe your valley as a dark valley. It was St. Peter who wrote, "Don't be surprised when you are tested by troubles or painful suffering, as if something unusual is happening to you" (1 Peter 4:12, TEV). You're going to face trouble at some point in your life. Jesus himself promised us in John 16:33 that while we live on planet Earth, we're going to have trouble. It's going to happen. But listen, he also said in the very next breath, "Take heart! I have overcome the world."

So yes, there will be trouble, but this trouble, regardless of how big or small, does not have to overcome us. How do we know this? Because Jesus has promised that *he* has overcome the world, and whatever comes our way out of the world does not match the matchless grace and goodness and strength and power of Jesus. That should be good news to hear!

King David wrote in Psalm 34 that ". . . the good man does not escape all troubles – he has them too." Great! Super encouraging, Paul. Thanks for sharing! Hold on.

Keep reading. Don't stop. He goes on in the very next line to say this: "But the Lord helps him in each and every one." Yes, you are going to have trouble. Yes, you are going to walk through dark valleys. Yes, the Lord will help you with each and every step through that dark valley. You need to know this, even if you learn nothing else from this little devotional.

I can relate to King David, the shepherd-boy-turned-king of Israel, who knew something about valleys. This guy understood loneliness, frustration, confusion, and disappointment along with physical, emotional, and spiritual valleys. He was a thinker, processor, and of course, a writer. Throughout the Psalms, he attaches language to the deepest valleys in life, and we can easily identify with his vulnerability and transparency. And while we see in the Scriptures so many good men and women of God sorting through failure, fear, conflict, and exhaustion, it was David who offered poetic license to cry out to God in an intimate and honest fashion, offering a model for us to follow what we can use as a template to do the same in our deepest and often darkest valleys.

Psalm 23 is no doubt his most remarkable and memorable contribution to literature. I'd like to drop anchor on this passage for a moment as we close out this devotional. I hope, in doing so, you find encouragement in your dark valley. Listen to David talk to God, praying to God about his dark valley. This is a very personal and intimate moment with God.

*The Lord is my shepherd; I have all that I need. He
lets me rest in green meadows; he leads me beside
peaceful streams. He renews my strength. He guides
me along right paths, bringing honor to his name.
Even though I walk through the darkest valley, I
will not be afraid, for you are close beside me!*
Psalm 23:1-4

There is so much to glean from this brief and very famous text; however, I want to focus on one phrase. David asserts that even though he has been walking through the darkest valley, he need not be afraid. Why? Because he has a firm belief that God was close beside him. "Even though I walk through the darkest valley, I will not be afraid, for you are close beside me!" (verse 4).

Even though I cannot see in the dark.

Even though I cannot trust fully in the dark.

Even though I don't know which hand to grab in the dark.

Even though I know that things are not going my way in the dark.

Even though I walk through the darkest valley, I will not be afraid.

I will not have eyes of fear, I will have eyes of faith. How can he write this with such confidence? David answers, **". . . for you [God] are close beside me."**

This little word grouping, *close beside me,* can be translated a couple of different ways. It can mean literally to be "beside me" or "within me," which would be enough to encourage my spirit in any dark valley. Knowing the God of the universe, who created all things and can control all things—should he choose to—is also a God who is right next to me and/or within me in my darkest hour, is mind-blowing. If you know that to be true, is that enough to give you the strength to persevere? I would hope so.

Hold on, though. There is more to this little phrase. It gets so much better!

This phrase "close beside me" could also be translated an additional way: *"to be bound to or obligated to."* That, in my darkest hour, not only is God beside me, holding my hand, but he is also within me, empowering me and giving me all that I need to be and all that I need in my moments of loneliness, confusion, frustration, and hurt. Additionally, this passage suggests that God is obligated to or bound to me in those moments of fear, loneliness, uncertainty, frustration, and confusion.

Don't hear what I'm not saying. *I'm not saying God owes you.* I'm not saying you earned anything to get into God's favor or to gain his helping you. I'm saying that there is a relationship available to you and me that is described as a covenantal relationship between us and God. That as we submit our lives to the rule and reign of a God who cares for us, pursues us, loves us, sacrifices for us, and gives all that He is to us—as we give Him our lives—He is ready to offer the resources of Heaven so that we can be everything we were made to be. In our darkest valleys, God is bound to us in this covenantal relationship.

The writer of Hebrews offers a promise that God will never leave us or forsake us (Hebrews 13:5). This is one strong promise amongst 3,000 promises in Scripture that orbit around God's fantastic pursuit of this relationship of his with you and me.

What does this really mean for you and me in our darkest valleys?

How can I really make sense of this valley? I'd like to offer something entirely practical in your very real season of pain, hurt, frustration, and disappointment. I'd like to offer three more promises gleaned from this idea that God is close to us in our darkest valleys. Here they are:

First, remember that you are not alone.

If God is close beside you, then you are not alone. I recognize I may sound redundant, but you need this reminder. So many times, in our seasons of fear, frustration, disappointment, or exhaustion, we forget that we are not alone as people of faith. When we are in these dark valleys, it's dark. Often, we cannot see what is right in front of us. We are so focused on what is happening to us that we cannot see what is next to us or who is next to us. No judgment zone here. It happens to each of us in the dark valleys. I once told a story about my daughter and me while in Mexico and our encounter with a rabid dog. She still felt fear even though she felt the physical touch of my hand. Even though she knew in her heart I was there with her, she also knew in her head there was something potentially greater outside of my protection. But what happened when that dog came charging in our direction? She experienced, in an instant, my impulse to protect her, my willingness to put myself in the way of danger so that her life would be saved. That is what a loving father does, whether his daughter fully understands it or not. How much more will our heavenly father do for us? In fact, he has done more . . . when he emptied himself into the form and frame of humanity (Jesus) and offered himself as the ransom price for our lives. He gave up his rights, his privilege, and his personal and eternal fortune, putting himself in the way of danger so that my life and your lives could be saved. I love the apostle Paul's language attached to this trust that says we cannot be separated from this kind of love.

> *And I am convinced that nothing can ever separate us from God's love. Neither death nor life, neither angels nor demons, neither our fears for today nor our worries about tomorrow—not even the powers of hell can separate us from God's love.*
> Romans 8:38

You are not alone. It may feel like it, but please know it is not your reality in the economy of a relationship with God. The Scriptures promise that nothing can ever separate us from God's love. Nothing. Our fears are real, but they do not have the power to disconnect us from God. They just don't.

Second, remember that God has a good purpose for your valley.

There is good purpose in our pain. I'm not saying that God brought this cancer into my life or this season of pain into your life. God doesn't necessarily cause dark valleys. Sometimes, the dark valleys happen because it's a dark and broken world. The reality reiterated in the Scriptures is that God is in the business of making opportunities out of obstacles. With eyes of faith, you can find purpose in the pain or the problem.

> *We can rejoice, too, when we run into problems and trials, for we know that they help us develop endurance. And endurance develops strength of character, and character strengthens our confident hope of salvation. And this hope will not lead to disappointment. For we know how dearly God loves us, because he has given us the Holy Spirit to fill our hearts with his love.*
> Romans 5:3-5

This is one of the more difficult realities to grasp in any season. This type of faith is like a muscle that needs to be developed, to be sure. Paul tells us that these seasons develop endurance, which develops strength of character, which develops a confident hope that we have been saved, are being saved, and will continue to be saved. This kind of hope, Paul reassures, will not disappoint. In fact, it will reassure us of God's love and remind us that God is alive and well and at work in our lives by way of the Holy Spirit. Not a bad Scripture to hold in our hearts, one packed with reassuring promises of God's goodness given in immeasurable portions.

But the reality is that we need help on this one. Sometimes, the Scripture is not enough for me. I'm just being honest. Sometimes, I need a human to encourage my heart, and this is where God's family comes into play because this is also how God works. He gets it. He understands that we need the physical touch or tangible encouragement, so he brings into our lives people who will walk beside us, encouraging us in various ways.

Outside of my wife and family, there were two guys from our small group who consistently pursued me daily, sometimes multiple times a day. They did so via texts, phone calls, and sometimes, random acts of service, such as dropping off comfort food like pizza and ice cream. They were just present, encouraging me in the reality that God is still here; God is still at work, and God is not finished with me yet.

God wants to invade and arrest your life. He wants to come alongside you, and not only to demonstrate that you are not alone, but God genuinely wants to reveal his purpose in your life. He'll do it through the Scriptures. He'll do it through a friend. He wants to take this difficult season, mold you and shape you, chip away all of the things that are not from him, and restock you with all of the things that are from him. Love. Joy. Peace. Patience. Kindness. Goodness. Faithfulness. Gentleness. Self-control. He wants to give you this fruit in your life. Mustering up such virtues certainly doesn't seem possible in this season, does it? That is the point of spiritual fruit. It doesn't come from with us alone. In the strength of God, according to Galatians 5:22, that he is willing to plant these seeds in us, filling us up again to nourish us back to the better and best version of ourselves—how we were meant to be.

Going through it or growing through it.

At the end of this day, you have to ask yourself this one question: *Will I go through this season, or will I grow through this season?* How you answer this question will change the trajectory of your entire life. It's a question I have constantly asked myself throughout this past year, and at the end of the day, I most consistently chose my best life for the rest of my life, but I didn't do it alone. God was speaking to me daily through his Scriptures, through agonizing prayer, and through the consistent comfort and care of my wife, my kids, my extended family, and a few God-sent friends.

Lean into what God would like to do in this season of your pain. Trust that the very better and best version of you is what is on his mind and on the other side of this season. In a relationship with Jesus, it can be your reality. You are not alone. There is purpose in this season of pain.

Finally, remember that this is only a chapter in your story.

This is not the end. This is just a chapter, and it's not the final chapter. It may be a frustrating and painful chapter or two or three. It may even be an undignified and embarrassing chapter in your life, but it's not the final chapter in your life. You need to know this. It's just a chapter and like any chapter in a book, the narrative is taking you somewhere. And believe it or not, this chapter has meaning and purpose if you will listen closely enough to find it. In fact, Scripture promises that there is even a reward that can be found in each chapter, regardless of the level of tragedy. That may sound offensive and asinine, but please keep reading just a bit longer as I offer an illustration.

I can remember learning how to waterski. Please know that I'm a terrible water skier, but the day that I got up on those skis, I had one phrase on my mind. The more experienced skiers had told me, "Do not let go when it gets tough on the turn." That phrase was planted in my brain, and I was rehearsing it as my six-foot, five-inch frame came up out of the water and began to ski for the very first time. I was surprised, elated, and terrified at the same time. With all of those emotions, I remembered the phrase: "I will not let go when it gets tough on the turn." I repeated it over and over as I anticipated the turn that would inevitably come my way.

My moment of truth was in front of me. The turn came. My ride got tough. It was hard to hold on as I went faster and faster around the turn. The rope got tighter and my strength got weaker and before I knew it, I bailed and went tumbling hard in what seemed like a hundred flip-flop turns out of the water and under the water. It hurt. I felt like someone punched me right in the middle of my face. As I surfaced, all I could remember was to hold my hand up high, letting surrounding boaters know I was in the water and needed to be rescued. What I hadn't realized was that in the fall, I completely lost my swimming shorts and was entirely naked with no knowledge of where those shorts were. A sad, funny, and sorry side story to the point I'm trying to make. Had I held onto the rope, I could have come around the difficult "valley" of the turn; I could have experienced the best in front of me. A humorous story to be sure but so relevant to our lives.

I would like to present the same teachable moment to anyone reading this little devotional. If you're not dead, God is not done. I don't mean to minimize this chapter in your life. It's tough. It's frustrating. It's painful. It's agonizing, and nobody would judge you for giving up. These seasons are often intolerable, unfair, frustrating, disappointing, and oh my gosh, I wish I had a big enough vocabulary to attach the many applicable words to your tragedy. However, the phrase we're getting to in this final thought is to *hang in there . . . with God*. I don't mean to sound cute, trite, or even simplified. The operative and key tag on an often cute phrase to "hang in there" is *with God*.

With God, all things are possible (Matthew 19:26).

With God, you can get in on what He is up to in and through your life.

With God, you can even travel beyond your own circumstances into service to others, even within your all-consuming pain and tragedy.

This is only possible when God invades your tragedy and stands up inside of you, animating you, and illuminating the better and best version of who you were made to be for the sake of someone else.

This is what God does.

The reward is union with God and all that he is and is doing in this world. Paul the apostle offers language that is poetic and pointed, "For our present troubles are small and won't last very long. Yet they produce for us a glory that vastly outweighs them and will last forever! So, we don't look at the troubles we can see now; rather, we fix our gaze on things that cannot be seen. For the things we see now will soon be gone, but the things we cannot see will last forever" (2 Corinthians 4:17–18).

God promises a reward for our faithfulness in our dark valleys. What we will experience in eternity is going to be so much greater than our present circumstances. No doubt. That is how the final chapter plays out. However, this is not where you are right now. The chapter you are in is certainly frustrating, to be sure, but don't miss the overall narrative that is in motion in your life. The best is yet to come for you.

- You are not alone in this season.
- There is purpose in this season.
- This is not the final chapter in this season.

God is present in your pain and God is *re*-presenting a new reality in your life, one that says doubt is not the opposite of faith; it is an element of faith. God is not surprised or overwhelmed by this season in your life. Even though you may be and probably are overwhelmed. My heart and encouragement for you in this book are very simple: You can trust him with your pain, suffering, uncertainty, frustration, and disappointment. Doubt is not wrong. It's what you do with your doubt that matters.

Remember, you can go through this season, or you can grow through this season. *You can be devout in your understandable doubt.* My prayer for you during your time of suffering is that you will develop humble confidence in this reality.

Peace and love to you.

Pastor Paul

———————◼—□—◼———————

Only in the darkness can you see the stars.
Dr. Martin Luther King, Jr.

Though my soul may set in darkness, it will rise in perfect light: I have loved the stars too fondly to be fearful of the night.
Sarah Williams

We are all broken, that's how the light gets in.
Ernest Hemingway

Scripture reading.

Even when I walk through the darkest valley, I will not be afraid, for you are close beside me.
Psalm 23:4a

Reflection.

Your darkest valley can be your deepest opportunity for growth. Your journey is not over. You may still be or will continue to see obstacles in your life—albeit physical, spiritual, emotional, or relational. Your question to answer is this: Will you go through this season or grow through this season? The way you answer this question will change the trajectory of your life.

Prayer.

God, as difficult as this season is, I don't just want to go through it, I want to grow through it. Give me eyes to see my obstacles as an opportunity to become the best and version of myself possible, not just for my sake but for the sake of those in my life. Amen.

SMALL GROUP QUESTIONS

This section is intended to assist discussion groups should they choose to walk through this devotional together. Anything that has happened of significance in our lives usually happens withing the context of relationship. We are better together when we process our life experiences within community.

A great format for any discussion group could follow as such:

1. **Pick a place**. Select a place where those in your group will be comfortable, feel at home, and don't mind hanging out a while. This place should have minimal distractions. If you can provide some food or a place where your people can grab food and/or a coffee or drink, even better. Then, Google some simple ice-breakers and find a quick question or two that will gather hearts and minds into one place.

2. **Read the entries (chapters).** These entries are short. Hopefully, your group members will have

come having already read the entries. It's a good idea to read through the chapter together so that everyone can dial up the concepts, ideas, and truths presented. It's good to have the entry fresh in their minds to have a good discussion.

3. **Facilitate the discussion.** It's important in any small group discussion to facilitate, meaning create a conversation, where it is easy for people to speak up, share, and wrestle with ideas they have. The idea in any small group is discovery, giving the Holy Spirit space to do his work within a community of skeptics, dreamers, and thinkers. Don't use this time to preach, teach, or tell people how they should think. Use this time and space to help your group members discover the messages that the Holy Spirit has for them, letting God do most of the heavy lifting.

I encourage you to keep the discussion informal and use the questions below as a guide for cultivating a space of discovery. You don't need to ask them in order. Just ask them as you feel led to ask them. These questions may even spark your own questions as follow-up.

Ten questions that will help you initiate good discussions in your small group.

- After reading through this entry, what is your first reaction?
- What do you think the key message of this chapter is? Explain why you think this.

- Which point of the entry spoke to you the most? Explain why you think so.
- Did you learn something new from this entry? Explain what it is?
- What did you discover about yourself in this entry?
- How did the Scripture verse relate to the letter and to your life?
- Is there an area of your life you feel you need to surrender to God? What is it and how would you feel about such a change?
- Was there an idea, principle, or truth presented that contradicts what you might hear in the world? If so, what is it?
- As a result of reading this entry, what changes do you think God would want you to make in your attitude, words, or actions?
- How could you encourage someone else from what you learned in this letter?

Pray together.

Spend time praying together. It won't be hard to come up with what or how to pray after your discussion. Simply pay attention to what is being said and pray over the discoveries, challenges, and victories. A great model to follow in prayer is ACTS:

- **A** – *Adore God.* Spend some time simply loving on God, telling him why he is so great and good in your life. Don't spend this time thanking him for what he has done for you just yet. Spend this time simply putting God in his rightful place as the God of the universe.

- **C** – *Confess to God.* Tell him about areas in your life that are out of alignment and need work, areas where you have taken control and where you know God needs to be in control.

- **T** – *Thank God.* Thank God for all of the many blessings in your life that you had nothing to do with. God is always at work showing up and showing off. Thank him for that work and those areas.

- **S** – *Surrender to God.* Spend this time surrendering any and all areas of life where you know you need God's help.

ACKNOWLEDGMENTS

This devotional was conceived in a season of suffering. While the writing of this project was one of the most painful processes in my life, the reality of this printed book just fell into place mainly due to the encouragement, love, and support of so many people cheering me on even when I didn't want to be on the field at play. There were days I simply wanted to give up and quit but the individuals mentioned in this section continued to text, email, call, and one some days, even in quarantine, actually physically showed up to push me back into the game. Was there doubt present in my life? Of course, there was. However, devotion is often developed within a deep community, and our strength is often enhanced on the shoulders of friends and a family of faith.

I will be forever grateful to Dr. Yuliya Linhares and the staff at the Miami Cancer Institute. From the housekeeping staff, nurses, technicians, oncologists, and various specialists, the level of competence, compassion, and care you give your patients is beyond anything I could have ever imagined. Thank you for saving lives every day, including my own.

To Pastors Kevin and Debbie Fischer and the staff and congregation at the Miami Vineyard Community Church. You have been so accommodating, patient, and loving these past couple of years and it has been a privilege to lead this team. Wherever I go, this faith family will hold a sacred place in my heart. I will always be cheering this community of Jesus followers on!

Thank you to everyone in the Morgan James publishing family who encouraged me and created a pathway to publishing that has been so personal and meaningful. You make it possible for individual stories to become collective stories memorialized to inspire generations. I'm grateful to you for taking a chance on me.

I am excited to include Terry Linhart on this page. A long-time youth pastor, professor, writer, speaker, and curator of ministry culture, you are genuinely the real deal. In the almost twenty years of friendship, you have constantly been a cheerleader to me and so many other practitioners, young and seasoned. You were the first person I approached with this idea, and you didn't hesitate to coach, encourage and connect me to Morgan James Publishing. Thank you for believing in me!

A very special "thank you" to PJ Ashenfelter. I can count on one hand the number of individuals that I would consider a lifetime friend. The mutual respect, encouragement, accountability, and brotherly love that we share are fuel for my soul.

I'm grateful to my family. To my parents, Andrea and Cliff Kerns, your knees must be sore praying for me for so many years. You have been patient and persistent in encouraging me to myself, nothing more and nothing less. Your children and grandchildren struck gold with you both! To my brothers Larry and Stephen Baldwin. When I was down, you picked me up. When I was up, you celebrated with me. When there was nothing to say, we joked, we goofed off, we laughed and laughed some more. I'm inspired and encouraged by your lives and love.

Finally, to my wife Becky and my children: Elizabeth, Elisha, Hannah, and Abigail. Next to my relationship with Jesus, you are the source and supply of life and love that is unmatched! I love you beyond words!

THANK YOU, READERS!

I am humbled that you picked this little devotional up and walked this journey with me.

My prayer has been and will continue to be that the inevitable doubt you will experience in your season of suffering will not diminish or even divide your faith. Rather, I'm hoping and praying that your doubt will lead you to a deeper dive of devotion in your faith walk. That was the goal of this devotional.

May the God of grace and peace give you all that you need to be all that you need to be in this next season of life. I'm cheering you on!

If I can be of further service to you on any level, I'd consider it a great honor to do so. I'm at your service. You can reach me at www.PaulBaldwin.org.

ABOUT THE AUTHOR

Paul Baldwin has been a pastor and leader for thirty years. His primary work has been investing in hungry leaders who have a deep desire to have a big kingdom impact in their immediate contexts. Paul holds an undergraduate degree in Sociology and Organizational Management and a Master's  Degree in Education and Counseling from Cal Poly State University. He is currently working on his Master's Degree in Global Leadership from Fuller Seminary. He has served as a consultant, coach, and church planter across the United States. For the past seven years, Paul has served as the executive pastor at the Miami Vineyard Church, a large multi-cultural faith community in southwest Miami, Florida. He leads a team of forty staff, 400 volunteers, and 4,000 members. He and his wife, Becky, have four children and live in Miami, Florida.

A free ebook edition is available with the purchase of this book.

To claim your free ebook edition:

1. Visit MorganJamesBOGO.com
2. Sign your name CLEARLY in the space
3. Complete the form and submit a photo of the entire copyright page
4. You or your friend can download the ebook to your preferred device

Print & Digital Together Forever.

Snap a photo

Free ebook

Read anywhere

CPSIA information can be obtained
at www.ICGtesting.com
Printed in the USA
JSHW021956090622
26899JS00001B/3